Classroom Management for Catechists

- ?? *Discipline strategies for building teacher confidence*
- ?? *Solutions for challenging situations*
- ?? *Sample classroom routine*

JENNIFER FITZ

Liguori
ONE LIGUORI DRIVE
LIGUORI MO 63057-9999

Imprimi Potest:
Harry Grile, CSsR, Provincial
Denver Province, The Redemptorists

Published by Liguori Publications
Liguori, Missouri 63057

To order, call 800-325-9521
www.liguori.org

Library of Congress Cataloging-in-Publication Data

Fitz, Jennifer.
    Classroom management for catechists / Jennifer Fitz.—First edition.
    pages cm
1. Classroom management—United States. 2. Christian education—United States. I. Title.
    LB3013.F527 2013
    371.102'4—dc23

                                                                    2012042555

pISBN: 978-0-7648-2234-6
eISBN: 978-0-7648-2308-4

Liguori Publications, a nonprofit corporation, is an apostolate of The Redemptorists. To learn more about The Redemptorists, visit Redemptorists.com.

Printed in the United States of America
17 16 15 14 13 / 5 4 3 2 1
First Edition

CONTENTS

ABOUT THE AUTHOR

 Jennifer Fitz has been teaching and writing since graduate school in the mid-1990s, but she never knew terror until she darkened the doors of a fifth-grade religious-education classroom. After her first spectacular failure, she learned the secret so many other teachers have uncovered: **It is possible to learn how to teach well, even if you don't naturally "just know" what to do.** In *Classroom Management for Catechists*, Jennifer explains the techniques of classroom behavior management as a series of skills and processes that anyone can learn and master.

When she isn't indulging her catechesis habit, Jennifer home-schools her four children, manages the Catholic Writers Guild blog, and escapes to play outside in her jungle of a garden. Find her online at AmazingCatechists.com, CatholicMom.com, NewEvangelizers.com, and at her personal blog, JenniferFitz.wordpress.com.

ACKNOWLEDGMENTS

This book exists thanks to my two directors of religious education, Donna Tomasini and Jackie Brace. They let me teach and they let me learn from my many mistakes.

I survived my first disastrous weeks as a catechist thanks to my online mentor, catechist, and schoolteacher Pamela O'Keefe. In my first years as a catechist, a small but vital part was played by public school teachers Alva Suggs and Dr. Chris Craft. Eternal thanks to Columbia Crossroads for letting me learn along with your Sunday school teachers when we prevailed on Dr. Craft to share his not-so-dark arts.

To my fellow catechists, Kathleen Doran, Linda Cadena, Karen Kays, and Daylin Silber, it has been a joy to teach alongside you. Matt Wilson, you rock. I give regular thanks for the tireless efforts of Sister Pamela Smith in forming and reforming us catechists.

A number of educators gave me feedback and guidance as I wrote, including Lisa Mladinich, Sarah Reinhard, Christian Le-Blanc, John McNichol, Dorian Speed, Mary Hathaway, Kathy Naso, Bob Weigold, Elaine Bonacci, Kelly Jacobs, and Father Patrick Toner. Writing help came from editor Christy Hicks of Liguori Publications, Sister Marie-Paul Curley, and the whole gang at the Catholic Writers Guild nonfiction critique group. I could never buy enough books to adequately thank Maureen Weigold at the Saint Francis Catholic Shop for her encouragement as I wrote.

The generosity of my family has made it possible for me to teach and write. Jon, Joshua, Evelyn, Eleanor, and Annelisa: You are more wonderful than I'd ever dared dream.

"...If mercy has been shown to me,
it is because Jesus Christ
meant to make me the greatest evidence
of his inexhaustible patience...."

1 Timothy 1:16

INTRODUCTION

WHAT IS CLASSROOM BEHAVIOR MANAGEMENT?

My first year teaching religious education was a disaster. My partner, Kathleen, and I tried to create a friendly atmosphere and inspired a room full of class clowns. What do you say when one of the boys requests you call him by the nickname "Cookie?" We offered hands-on learning activities and reaped chaos. The insect crawling out from the nature items for the prayer table didn't help. But the lowest point amid all the craziness of our first few weeks was seeing a student rejected and isolated when she didn't fit in with the cliques on the playground. Parents called to complain.

How could this happen to us? We loved the kids, loved to teach, and loved sharing our faith. These were curious, lively, friendly children coming from loving Christian homes. We had a supportive director of religious education (DRE) and all the educational resources we could want. The ingredients for a great religious-education program were all in place.

But as with cooking, there is a science—and an art—to combining the ingredients. We couldn't just toss everything into the pot and expect soup. We had to learn methods for creating order—and education—out of the chaos.

These methods are what professional teachers call "classroom management." It's a code phrase that means, "the things I do to get these banshees to settle down and concentrate so I don't run away screaming and never set foot in the classroom again." Or, put differently, the way to get parents to stop calling to complain about my class...and maybe even start calling to say how much their students love it.

The good news is that classroom behavior management is a specific set of skills anyone can learn and master. No matter how crazy and out of control your class feels right now, you can turn it around. And because you'll understand how the different tools and approaches work, you'll know how to assess new problems and choose the responses most likely to help.

The techniques in this book are nothing new or revolutionary. These are time-tested methods that work in all kinds of classrooms. In teaching myself to manage classroom behavior, I started with the experts. I read books on classroom management written for professional teachers. I pulled aside teacher friends and picked their brains for ideas and help. At one point I begged Dr. Christopher Craft—a middle-school teacher and nationally recognized expert on learning and student behavior—to teach a workshop for Sunday school teachers. Among other things, he taught us the importance of using classroom routines—both the neurology behind it and practical tricks like what to do when students arrive late to class.

With some aggressive coaching and a lot of practice, our class was transformed. One student told her mother at year-end, "Mom, this was my favorite year of religious ed because I learned so much about the faith."

I know I'm not the only catechist who has struggled with class-room discipline. What has surprised me, though, is the response I have received from the professional teachers I asked to review the book. A public high-school teacher confided, "I think too often teachers are taught content, various wonderful lesson plans, etc., but we are never taught basic classroom management!" Catholic middle-school teacher and author John McNichol said simply, "I wish I could have read this before I started my teaching career."

The basic principles of classroom behavior management are the same whether you are teaching high-school algebra or a group of kindergartners at vacation Bible school. But while I imagine this book will help many full-time professional teachers, I've written it specifically for the parish catechist. As we walk through the methods and tools of classroom management, we'll be looking at how to apply them to the distinctive challenges and requirements of a religious-education program. Let's start by taking a look at the types of situations we catechists can expect.

1

YOUR WORLD AS A CATECHIST

How would you describe a "typical" Catholic religious-education program? Yours might be a tiny mission parish with just a handful of children and a single catechist who plays teacher, DRE, and hall monitor for them all. Or maybe you attend a mega-parish with religious-education programs running five nights a week and a parish secretary who dreams of a simpler life doing something relaxing for a change—maybe air-traffic control or managing Penn Station.

Some of the challenges in teaching religious education will be unique to your parish. Other problems—and advantages—are familiar to many if not all religious-education programs. Let's start by talking about you, the teacher, and then we'll look at the other factors that impact your work as a catechist.

Who Teaches Religious Education?

Volunteers and amateurs. Every now and then you find a catechist with formal professional training in both education and theology, but it's relatively rare. Most of us are self-taught and learn on the job. As a catechist you'll discover that one of the most powerful classroom-management techniques is simply to teach an interesting course: Students behave better when they aren't bored. Don't let a lack of training or experience discourage you. Instead, recognize the gifts you bring to the classroom—whether it's a passion for art, or experience dealing with a difficult life situation, or a bubbly personality, or just a love for your students and a desire to help them know Jesus. Seek out the training or help you need to improve on your weaknesses, but don't be afraid to be creative in sharing your faith in ways unique to you and the person God made you to be.

Who's Helping You?

Good safe-environment practices call for a team approach. There's a chance you've lucked into the perfect partners, but don't lose heart if you have to work through disagreements or misunderstandings. Chapter 7 is focused entirely on how to work with your teaching partners to build a well-rounded, satisfying class that draws on each of your strengths. Depending on your parish, your helpers might be teens who require firm coaching or parent volunteers who don't wish to take an active role in the classroom. You may find yourself teaching solo, with an open door and adult backup somewhere down the hallway. Have a backup plan in case your expected help falls through at the last minute.

Throughout the book, there are times when I say something along the lines of "have a helper do..." or "ask an assistant to...," and it's possible you have no such help on hand. What to do? When you're teaching solo, you have no choice but to hone your leadership skills. In the classroom, look for ways your students can help you—for example, pairing students for activities so they can work together and assist each other or having student volunteers take charge of classroom chores. But emergencies and disruptions happen. If you have no assistant who can take responsibility for the class, you must work with your DRE or pastor to agree on an action plan for how to handle these situations. The particulars of your facility, the age of your students, and the presence of other adults in the building will determine the safest way to respond to student emergencies.

Where Will You Teach?

Parish facilities vary dramatically, but few catechists inherit their dream classroom. I've taught with artfully arranged buckets collecting rain from a leaky roof, an arsenal of electric fans strategically aimed to keep students conscious when the air-conditioner broke on a 98-degree day, and of course the one thing I dread more than a broken photo-copier: no dry-erase markers. (I now keep an emergency supply of markers and chalk in my backpack at all times.) We'll talk about ways you can manage the classroom (or lack-of-classroom) environment in chapter 2, and what steps to take to reduce the chance of unexpected disaster in chapters 3 and 8. When it comes to classroom equipment, it pays to pack a sense of humor. You'll need it.

What Kind of Textbooks, Supplies, and Other Resources Will You Have?

Let's be clear: You will not be given a perfect curriculum nor all the supplies you wish you could have. Your parish has to operate within a tight budget and balance a wide variety of needs. And no matter how faithfully you follow the script in the teacher's manual, your students have not been properly coached to respond on cue. This can be frustrating, not only because you don't care for that exercise on page 37, but because a mismatch between the program and the students can be a source of behavioral problems.

Nothing is more stressful than feeling like you can't teach the course you are expected to teach. Assume the best about your DRE and your pastor (it's highly unlikely they are intentionally trying to make you miserable), and work with them to find ways to make the resources you do have work as well as possible. Ask what supplies are available, where they are kept, and what the policy is for using them. Find out what the teaching priorities are for your class and to what extent you may adapt or modify the curriculum. When problems arise, explain the difficulty you are having, share the solution you'd like to try, and then ask for feedback. Because many catechists work with a purely imaginary budget, throughout the book we'll look for zero-cost ways to work with any curriculum to solve common challenges in religious education.

What Kind of Course Are You Teaching?

During the school year, you may be teaching a fairly academic course, often meeting for about an hour a week. In the summer you might be volunteering for an intensive week-long vacation program or one that meets for several hours an evening over the course of a month. Perhaps you've been co-opted as a volunteer for a one-day-only holiday program during Advent or Easter. You might be the substitute for someone else's course or find yourself teaching double or triple your expected number of students because another volunteer called in sick. Effective planning is the key to a successful course, so much so that we'll spend the second half of this book learning how to build plans that help you teach effectively. But here's the best part: By learning how to plan thoroughly when you have the luxury of doing so, you'll also develop the ability to respond on the fly as surprises come your way.

Who's Coming to Your Class?

The types of problems you encounter will depend in part on your students' maturity. Younger students have shorter attention spans, less self control, and more physical energy. Chapter 4 focuses on strategies for teaching very young or energetic students. Throughout the book we'll explore problems and solutions that arise among different age groups, and I'll note which approaches work best for whom. In chapter 6 we'll see how to address a few very disconcerting behavioral problems that can occur in a religious-education setting. The good news is that with patience and graciousness, you can help even your most reluctant students experience the love of Christ.

Nearly every religious-education class can count on one particular difficulty: You will have students who have just darkened the doors of the church for the first time ever and others who know the faith so well they could teach your class for you. Chapter 5 explains a simple, flexible method for planning a class that is helpful and informative for all your students.

What Is the Parish Classroom Culture?

Asked how he manages classroom discipline, catechist and author Christian LeBlanc answered simply, "I well remember the childhood frustration of trying to learn while the teacher tolerated disruption. I won't stand for it at all. I give sixth-graders about 1.5 chances to not be disruptive. Then they are out of class to either sit in the DRE's office or sit in another class. They dislike both and are no trouble when they come back." In a parish culture built around a strong sense of discipline and order, a unified, no-nonsense approach to classroom discipline can make a catechist's life much simpler. Where the atmosphere is more relaxed and informal, teachers must develop their classroom-management skills to a greater degree. But good teaching will always win the hearts and minds of students. It does no good to take advantage of strict parish discipline only to bore students into offering up their suffering. A catechist like Christian LeBlanc insists on good behavior, yes; but his skill as an instructor brings students back to class wanting another chance. For this reason, a book devoted to classroom behavior management is also a book devoted to the art of teaching well.

You've volunteered as a catechist because you want to share Christ with your students. But first you've got to get these kids to settle down and listen! Let's start by diving into the elements of discipline: the six building blocks for creating a peaceful class environment that enables you to connect with your students and set the stage for effective teaching.

2

THE ELEMENTS OF DISCIPLINE

How do I get these kids to behave?! It's a question we may struggle with as parents, and it's no less a problem in the classroom. There can be no lesson if students are not able to focus on learning.

Some teachers have a natural leadership presence—they walk into a room, students behave, problem solved. I wish I had that magic, but I don't. And there's nothing more frustrating than having a fellow teacher or staff member say, "Well, just make them behave!" as if calming a roomful of rambunctious children were as simple as remembering to pay the water bill or feed the dog every morning.

If you're like me, vague admonitions to "stay on task" or "plan ahead" don't really mean much. Stay on what task? And I made a plan—why isn't it working? Natural leaders may not be aware of what it is they do so well because they just do it automatically.

But just because you and I don't magically know how to manage classroom behavior doesn't mean we're doomed to a life of pencil wars and paint on the walls. We can choose to learn how to use the tools of good discipline as part of an active strategy to make our class run as smoothly as possible.

Meet the Six E's

In order to think strategically about discipline, I organized what I call the "Elements of Discipline" into six E's: Example, Environment, Engagement, Explanation, Enforcement, and Encouragement. We're going to look at each one of them in detail.

One of the challenges of classroom discipline is choosing methods that are both effective and appropriate in the classroom setting. Certain types of discipline that are an important part of parenting may be ineffective or harmful when used by a teacher. As we walk through the six elements, we'll look at some specific actions that work well and some traps to avoid.

As you tackle behavioral problems in your classroom, ask yourself: Which element is needed here? What's missing? When faced with a new situation, you might not know exactly how to respond. Ask yourself what type—what category—of change is needed. Do students need me to set a better example? Did I fail to explain what I expected? Is there a distracting environment I can modify to make it easier to behave? Once we've identified the types of changes we need to make, it's easier to choose specific actions that are likely to help.

ELEMENT #1

Set the Right Example

Human beings are created to learn from one another. We naturally adopt the language, ideas, manners, and habits of the people around us, even without thinking about it. As a teacher, I need to make sure I'm using that copying instinct to teach my students how to behave well.

Consider the example you are setting for your students, both in and outside of class. Are your students struggling with their behavior in part because of what they are learning from you? Is it possible that your own struggle with some aspect of Christian life has caused you to give up on your ideals—and students are following your pattern? Let's do a quick Catechist's Examination of Conscience.

Catechist's Examination of Conscience

Do I take my religious-education class seriously? Do I come to class prepared, with my materials organized and a plan in place? Do I stay focused during class time, or am I tempted to chat with the other adults during class hours? I can't expect my students to be serious about class if I myself don't treat my class as a serious commitment.

Do I treat others with respect? Am I kind? Do I control my temper? Do I avoid sarcasm and gossip? Do I show respect for others both in what I say and in how I say it? Do I give others the benefit of the doubt or do I always assume the worst?

Am I devoted to prayer and the sacraments? What kind of example do I set at Mass and during prayer times in class? Am I reverent and respectful? Do I pray, sing, and receive Communion attentively and devotedly? Are my students likely to see me in line for the sacrament of confession?

How committed am I to my own faith? Am I doing my best to live out my Christian vocation all week long? Do I make a serious effort to cultivate my prayer life, to serve others, and to learn more about the faith? Have I given up on holiness, or have I made it my goal to keep cooperating with the grace of God until I get there?

What I do sends a powerful message: *This is how Christians behave. This is how you should behave.* Sobering, isn't it?

But wait a minute! *I'm still a long way from being a model Catholic.* Maybe you aren't 100 percent perfect either. Does this mean we shouldn't be catechists? No, usually not. But it does mean this: I need a Savior. And that's good news, because my students do, too. I can use my own failures as an opportunity to show my students how to apologize, how to ask for forgiveness, and how to make amends for my sins.

As a catechist, it's important I remember that humility and holiness are two sides of the same coin. Humility doesn't consist of setting low standards and resigning myself to being something less than holy. It consists of recognizing what holiness looks like in my state of life and being honest about where I still have some growing to do. In many cases, I stand side by side with my students, sharing the same struggles they face. The important thing is that we don't look at our own weaknesses and decide that's good enough. Instead, I need to point them to Christ, and we can look together toward him as our model and goal.

ELEMENT #2

Create an Environment That Makes It Easy for Students to Behave

It's a Friday during Lent, and you're starving. You open the fridge. There's a piece of leftover steak, a box of fried chicken, and a brand-new package of your favorite cold cuts. How easy is it going to be to keep that rule about no meat on Fridays? Not so easy. We do ourselves a favor if we empty the fridge of the stuff we're supposed to avoid and fill it with better options.

The classroom is the same way. We help our students by creating an environment that makes it easier to behave from the moment they walk in the door. Sometimes you will be able to prepare your teaching space before class begins. In other situations, you will have to quickly assess the room and make a snap decision about how to make the most of the setting you've been given. Cultivate the habit of identifying potential distractions, obstructions, and annoyances, and of finding ways to eliminate them when possible.

Match the physical environment to the activity. You can't always control this, but do your best. Is it possible to dim the lights for meditative prayer? Can you shut the classroom door to keep out noise from the hallway? Use background music selectively—make sure it is a help and not a distraction.

Sometimes you have to be creative to work around an unchangeable situation. Our parish gym is a giant echo chamber. Once you add thirty restless children, there is no hope of being able to teach a lesson everyone can hear. If we plan to use the gym for games, we first gather the students in another, quieter location where we can give instructions and answer questions.

Decide ahead of time where and how your students will pray. Standing is a reverent way to do a short set of opening and closing prayers, but sitting works better for long prayer sessions, especially meditative prayers. You may wish to gather everyone around a prayer table. Is there room to do so? Will the process of getting to and from the prayer station take more time than the prayer itself? Walk it out ahead of time and adjust your plans as needed.

Use seating arrangements to your advantage. Easily distracted students need to sit front and center, close to the teacher. This helps them stay focused on the lesson and helps you monitor any soon-to-erupt situations. High-energy students are often helped by doing extra classroom chores such as passing out papers, so having them at hand makes it easier to put them to work.

All students benefit from sitting near neighbors who help them stay focused on their work. Observe and use your judgment. Sometimes allowing best friends to sit next to each other means constant chatter and notes sent back and forth. But it can also mean a team of students who help each other stay on track or engage in friendly, productive competition for good grades.

Pay attention to the friendships, jealousies, and rivalries among your students. If you see a student being left out, rearrange to give that student a compatible tablemate. Both out of kindness, and to prevent the inevitable explosion, don't try to force a friendship between two students who obviously annoy each other or whose personalities are clearly at odds.

Give students the proper amount of space for the activity under way. Move students farther apart from each other during test-taking or meditative prayer. Put students closer together when they need to share books or work on a group project. When rearranging, teens may be able to choose their own spaces, but younger students will need guidance. Plan to actively assist students for any direction such as "get into groups of four" or "find a partner."

Use visual and physical cues to communicate expectations. If you need children to sit in a circle, use masking tape X's to show them where to sit or set out rugs and direct them to find one. If you want students to focus on a particular part of the room, arrange desks and chairs so that students are naturally looking in that direction. When showing a video, make sure all students can see and hear clearly.

Set up the room in a way that accommodates all students. If the arrangement of the room makes it impossible for a student with a disability to fully participate in class, or the planned activities exclude a student, plan again. If you aren't sure of your student's needs and abilities, ask. See chapter 6 for specific ways to meet the needs of students with disabilities.

Remove temptations. How would you feel if your friends welcomed you to their home, showed you to a comfortable seat, and placed a giant tray of freshly baked brownies in front of you— only to scowl and stamp feet if you dared to taste one? Students likewise assume that whatever items you place on their desk or table are meant for them and will naturally help themselves. They may "get to work" in ways you had not anticipated, unless you give clear instructions on when and how the supplies are to be used. Particularly tempting items should be stowed out of sight when not in use. If you bring interesting visual aids or props, keep them put away except when you want students to look at them.

You can use the power of distraction to your advantage by displaying or leaving within reach the items you want students to explore. Bibles, a crucifix, the words of a prayer displayed on a poster—these "distractions" are lessons in themselves—especially with older students, for there will be times when you need to teach material that some students have already mastered. Consider discreetly allowing advanced students to read from their Bible, work on an assignment, or read the textbook silently. When you again need all eyes up front, direct students to close their books, stack them in the center of the table, or stow them under their desks.

Your parish may have a policy on cell phones and other electronic devices. If you collect student phones during class time, make sure that the dismissal routine includes "The Returning of the Phones" as a specific checklist item. I find it effective to have a clearly marked "Cell Phone Prison" (a brightly colored shoe box) near the door, but to let students know that as long as I don't see or hear their digital device, I would rather they kept the device themselves—turned off and stored in a book bag or pocket.

Take care of drink and restroom breaks at designated times. If possible, have students go to the bathroom before they come into class. If your class lasts long enough that a second restroom break is needed, plan one into your schedule. This is a good time for students to work on independent activities such as a craft, worksheet, or journal.

Use "rhythm and routine" to map out a workable plan for your class. We'll delve into the details of this in the next chapters, but here's a preview of the three big ideas: (1) choose engaging activities appropriate for your students' ages and abilities; (2) order your activities so that the class runs smoothly; and (3) use routines to help students know what to expect and when to expect it.

This isn't an exhaustive list! Keep your eyes open for situations that are distracting to your students. Sometimes you can eliminate the distraction, sometimes you have to work around it. But to the best of your ability, make it as easy as possible for your students to behave.

ELEMENT #3

Students Should be Engaged in a Specific Activity at All Times

This is in many ways part of "Environment," but it is so important it deserves an "E" of its own. Here's a rule you can count on 100 percent of the time:

**If your students have nothing to do,
they will think up something to do.**

Plan your class so there is a steady flow of activities, including some extra tasks for students who finish work early.

"Keep them busy" does not mean entertaining students with a circus and acrobats! Classroom keep-me-busy activities include additional assignments, silent reading, cleaning up supplies, or praying a formal prayer with the help of a holy card or prayer booklet. But always have something for your students to do, and give clear instructions on what that something is.

Because effective planning is such an important part of classroom discipline, we'll be spending the next several chapters walking through the details of how to build a class that eliminates pockets of idle time. Sometimes, however, you the catechist will not be able to control your class schedule. You may find yourself stuck, sitting and waiting. Perhaps there's a special presentation about to begin, but the presenter is five minutes late. Or your class was supposed to meet the deacon in the church halfway through the class period, but the previous group of children is still finishing up, and you've got twenty-five kids jammed in the vestibule waiting their turn. If you don't quickly think of something to fill those five minutes, there will be a game of tag under way before you can say, "Quit playing with the choir robes!"

It's your job to be the leader. Pick a no-supplies-required, open-ended activity. This could be anything: Lead the class in impromptu prayers for pets, family members, and upcoming tests at school; play I Spy or Twenty Questions; quiz the kids on Bible trivia, or lead them in a discussion that allows them to share short answers to fun questions about themselves. If you have a talent for music or puppet shows, now's the time to lead the class in song or whip out the finger puppets and perform. This is also a great time to take open questions about the faith. Even if you don't know the answer, you can make a note of the question and follow up later.

Can an Old-Fashioned Catechist Compete in a Digital World?

There's much hand-wringing in religious-education circles these days about how to hold the attention of children who spend their days flitting from one high-tech activity to the next. Is it necessary for catechists to have the latest teaching technology? It's the rare parish that can match the digital amenities students find at school and home.

Let this be your secret weapon. Instead of trying to fit in with the digital crowd, stand out by offering human interaction—a chance for students to learn and explore in the real world, using their own imaginations, sharing their own ideas, and being given the attention of an adult who cares about them and is eager to listen and to share real-life experiences.

Be careful, though, as you find ways for students take an active role in class, to resist the temptation to let students run the class. You the adult should lead most activities—you have the knowledge, presentation skills, and sense of timing that lets you keep the class moving as you respond to student cues. Limit student presentations to about five minutes of class time per session. That's ten second-graders showing off their baptism pictures, five fifth-graders giving you their saint's top three facts, or two high school students sharing what they did for their service project over spring break. Give just enough time for students who long for some limelight to show their stuff, but not so long that you've exhausted the patience of the classmates politely doodling in their journals while they wait for the more polished teaching to resume.

ELEMENT #4

Students Need Clear Explanations of What You Expect

No one is born knowing exactly how to do everything. Even simple skills like taking turns or saying "please" and "thank you" must be taught. And once we have learned what to do, sometimes we need reminders. As a catechist, you will have to explicitly teach your students what you expect in your classroom. You will also sometimes have to coach students on social norms that you think they should already know. In the next chapter, we'll look at the importance of using standard procedures, or classroom routines, to simplify your class time. Right now let's look specifically at concerns about misbehavior.

Don't wait for students to misbehave before you begin communicating your expectations. At the beginning of the school year, *have the students develop a list of classroom rules.* Building their own list reminds them that they do understand the basics of good behavior and gives them ownership of the rules so that they think: *These aren't just my teacher's rules, these are my rules.*

As the students compose the rules, avoid overload. Show them how many small rules add up to a few guiding principles. "No scribbling in your book," "no drawing on the desks," and "no chewing up all the erasers" can all be combined as a single rule: "We will take care of our equipment and supplies." Copy the final list onto a poster board so that students have a visual reminder of the rules that they themselves made. All members of the class—students and teachers—then sign their names at the bottom of the poster as a pledge to keep the agreed-upon rules.

When you are teaching a single class session, such as for a special event or as a substitute teacher, you won't have the luxury of creating a class rules list. You may wish to open your class with a short rule-review reminder, such as, "We're going to get started now. Please remember that we will need to sit quietly and raise hands so that everyone has a turn to speak." If the class begins to get out of hand, pause the lesson and take a rule-review break.

Before praying, review appropriate behavior during prayer time. At the start of the year, lead students through several minutes of active discussion on how to behave while praying. You may want to prescribe a specific posture appropriate to the type of prayer you are doing. *Hands folded? Head bowed? Or eyes on a prayer card or crucifix?* Demonstrate respectful handling of rosary beads—children will play with them as they would with any rope, string, or necklace, unless you tell them otherwise. Many students need to be reminded to keep both feet on the floor and not to rock in the chair or sway precariously toward neighbors.

Throughout the year, students will need to be reminded of prayerful behavior. You might say, "Now we are going to pray.

Let's take a moment to quiet down and focus on Jesus. We'll put down our pencils, put our hands in our laps, and sit very still." Mention any specific challenges to prayer that hinder your particular class. For example, if your students are prone to poking each other during prayer time, you might say, "We are going to keep our hands to ourselves and respect each person's circle of private space."

When explaining to children how to act or how to do an assignment, you will often need to provide a physical model. If you are explaining how to move or speak, use your own body or voice to show how it is done. If you are explaining how to do a written assignment, either put a sample on the board or make a paper handout.

Be specific and give your students a precise example of exactly what is expected. If your student grabs or makes a rude demand, your admonishing, "Ask nicely" is too abstract. What exactly is "nicely?" Maybe the student thought he *was* being nice. Try this instead: *In our class we say, "May I have the pencil, please?"*

For younger students, exaggerate your intonation so they hear the changes in pitch of a polite request. Your student may choose to mimic your exact words or to offer some acceptable variation ("please, can I have it"), but in either case, you've equipped your student to be able to succeed.

Don't take ignorance as an insult—or use it as an excuse to embarrass. Some children figure out good manners all on their own; others have to be explicitly and repeatedly taught. That is why you have been privileged to assist them on their journey to adulthood. Children are also endlessly creative. Do not be the least surprised if you must explain such finer points as, "No putting your feet on people's heads," "You may not mark your page by sitting on your book," and, "We do not add sound effects to the Hail Mary."

It does not matter whether your student already knows that crayons don't belong in ears or is getting this information for the very first time. When you identify a problem behavior, simply tell your student what the appropriate action is. The calmer and less dramatic your delivery, the more you will be taken seriously. If the student was trying to get attention, the last thing you want to do is to act excited, outraged, amused, or astonished.

Be sensitive to embarrassment. Even your class clown will be hurt and mortified if reprimanded unexpectedly. When you must correct, do so gently, remembering that you, too, sometimes goof up or don't know the right thing to do. When one student is obviously out of sync with typical age-group behaviors, it is better to address problems privately.

Be aware that children do not have a finely tuned sense of proportion. The same child who thinks nothing of punching his neighbor continuously throughout the entire class period might break into tears if the directions say "use a purple crayon" and all he has to choose from in his crayon box are lavender and blue-violet. Children need to be told, "This is an important rule, here's why." And likewise, "It's OK if you don't do this assignment exactly," or, "You aren't in trouble if you don't finish this paper in time."

How Strict Do the Rules Need to Be?

One of the difficulties in teaching children how to behave and in establishing expectations for the classroom is that adults have very fluid rules. In the classroom, we call out answers, interrupt the instructor with questions, or quietly confer with other students. We observe formal manners in some situations and very casual manners in others. As a new teacher—or new to the age group you are teaching—you may not have a clear idea of what kinds of rules are needed to maintain order and respect in the classroom.

None of us wants to be stricter than necessary. Know that with most groups of elementary-aged students, you will need to be firm about requiring students to raise their hands and wait to be called upon. If you sense the class can handle more adult-like freedom (even some adults cannot), test it out by engaging in open discussion for a short time. If you do have times when students are not required to raise hands, be clear about telling the class whether this is "raise your hand" time, "call it out" time, or "group conversation" time.

Students of the same age still vary in their maturity and energy level. You may need to make hard and fast rules for one particular class of students on account of the personalities gathered in that group. For example, you might have initially allowed students to work as teams on a particular assignment. Only for whatever reason, these kids "discuss" at noise levels requiring industrial hearing protection. They don't know the meaning of "quiet down" or "use your inside voice." So for this one class, you have to make a "no talking during homework time" rule.

ELEMENT #5

Enforce the Rules

You cannot control your students. You cannot. You can vigorously encourage the right behavior, but at the end of the day (and religion is often taught at the end of the day), human beings are endowed with natural freedom. What you can control is your own reaction to your students' behaviors. Enforcement of the rules is that moment when you show you are committed to maintaining a respectful and peaceful classroom.

Remember that anger and drama on your part only escalate conflict. But you cannot simply ignore small-scale misbehavior in the hope it will go away. Let's look at some ways to calmly respond to common situations before they get out of hand.

Students are chatting during class. I walk over and stand next to them while I continue to teach. *I probably don't need to say anything at all.* My presence alone tells them, "I hear you, I am listening, and this is not acceptable."

Two students are passing notes during class. I pick up the note and put it in my pocket. *I probably don't need to say anything at all.* My action alone tells them, "I saw that, it is not acceptable, I will not allow it to continue." Do not read the confiscated note aloud to the class. This is embarrassing and disrespectful to your guilty students, and it disrupts the class. Your other students are here to learn about Christ, not about who thinks which boy is cute. Drama begets drama. If you start acting out in class by embarrassing misbehaving students, your class will learn from you and do the same.

The class is about to watch a video, and some students get fidgety during movies. Post a sign reminding students they must sit quietly during the movie. For younger students, do a quick rule review before the movie begins: *Do we wiggle during the movie or do we sit still? Do we talk and make noises or do we watch quietly with no sounds? Do we touch other people or keep our hands to ourselves? If you need to ask the teacher a question, what do you do?* Inform students that those who are unable to sit quietly may do a homework assignment in the hallway instead.

A student is mindlessly tapping on the desk with a pencil, distracting others. Pause and say, "Please stop tapping." Then resume teaching. A simple, calm request is enough to signal that you have a rule and that you intend to enforce it. If the student persists (it is very hard to control a fidgety habit), you can quietly take the pencil away until it is time to write. Be aware that some students need movement. Allow them to substitute a silent motion, such as tapping a finger in the palm of the opposite hand. Also, look for ways to add more physical activity to the curriculum.

Quiet, simple ways of communicating your seriousness to students are the foundations of discipline. When necessary, you can take your action to the next level:

○ Separate students who are talking or misbehaving together.
○ Remove temptation. Take away supplies or objects that students are damaging or using to bother others.
○ Direct a misbehaving student to sit in a chair against the wall, away from the regular seating area.
○ Require students who create noise and distraction during a movie to sit in the hallway and work on written assignments.

With very young students, you may need to prescribe one action in order to achieve another. To stop students from poking each other, give a direction such as "clasp your hands" or "put your hands on your knees" for some "hand time-out." If a student is kicking (children often kick their feet without knowing it), instruct the child to put his feet on the line on the floor, make his toes touch the carpet, or sit cross-legged. Remember to stay focused on your goal and to avoid a contest of wills. As long as the child chooses some acceptable way of controlling the wayward body part, it does not have to be exactly the way you suggested.

If the student turns your instruction into a game—for example by inching his toes along the carpet and toward his neighbor—you have a different kind of problem on your hands. The short-term enforcement response is to have the child sit away from the other students, or if necessary, take a time-out visit to the hallway or DRE's office. But the underlying problem is that the student wants to engage your attention—which is great news because you're the leader. Take a look at chapter 4 for interactive, high-energy ways to engage young children in the lesson. In the meantime, keep your own reaction bored and indifferent, and direct your attention toward students who are behaving appropriately.

A firm response to continued, intentional disruption sets the tone for the whole class. Veteran catechist Elaine Bonacci uses a magnet board with name tags to track each student's behavior. When students misbehave, they receive one warning. If the misbehavior continues, the student moves his name tag to the "warning" column of the magnet board. The third time the student misbehaves, he receives the agreed-upon consequence, such as being sent to the DRE's office.

Christian LeBlanc teaches older students and agrees on the importance of insisting on mutual respect: "If I have someone disrupting class, and being nice doesn't work on them...I tell them I will not allow them to interfere with other kids learning." The disruptive student is either sent to the DRE's office or directed to sit in another class. "I have thrown out less than one kid per year. They always have returned to class with improved behavior."

Note that a "firm response" does not mean hysterics and threats. It means communicating expectations clearly, then following through on reasonable consequences for the type and severity of the misbehavior. The student is received back to class graciously. If you have students with behavioral disorders, see chapter 6 for ideas on how to set reasonable standards and to accommodate the student's genuine inability to behave in an age-appropriate manner.

Taming the Talkers:
Techniques for Quieting Down a Noisy Class

What do you do when your class is just plain chatty? They aren't trying to cause trouble, they just have a lot to say and a powerful urge to say it. Ironically, it is often the most interesting classes that cause students to talk too much—they are excited about the course, and their enthusiasm bubbles over. Your class can learn how to settle down quickly through a combination of clear communication and practice following your cues.

At the beginning of the school year or the start of the course, teach students your signal for silence. You might explain to your students that when you raise your hand, that is the sign that they should stop talking. Once they know the signal, practice it. Have the students chat to each other for a few seconds, then raise your hand in the quiet signal. You can use this exercise in preparation for prayer as well. Have students practice switching on command from noisy to silent, from active to still, from busy to prayerful.

Sometimes students will get completely wound up and you may sense that a fresh restart will help. If so, let the students know you are going to stop everything and start over. Dim the lights if you can, and instruct students to lay their heads on their desks if you think that will help them; then have the class practice being completely silent and still for thirty seconds. It may take several rounds of practice before everybody stays still the full thirty seconds. Ask the class to confirm by a silent show of hands that they are ready to resume the lesson in a calm and respectful manner.

Over the longer-term, if your class is constantly chattering out of control, ask yourself if there are elements of the class that need to be revamped. Do the students have a chance to share and talk at appropriate times? Do they move through a variety of activities appropriate to their age and energy level? Do you have a consistent routine that makes the class session predictable? Are you teaching new and interesting material so that students aren't bored by the same lessons repeated year after year? For a naturally talkative class, choose learning activities that allow students to share and discuss. Group projects, short-answer discussions, and memorization shout-outs (see chapter 4) can give students a chance to learn-by-talking during class time.

Dead Ends: Enforcement Responses to Avoid

There are two areas where catechists need to tread carefully. The first is prayer: Is there a proper way to use prayer in response to student misbehavior? The second is apologies: Can I insist on an apology from a misbehaving student? Both of these can be part of a powerful response to student misbehavior, but both can just as easily sink the class into serious spiritual problems and emotional turmoil.

We'll start with prayer, because the answer is very easy: Never use prayer as a punishment. To do so is an utter abuse of a great gift. But when the class is having a difficult time behaving, it may be appropriate to halt the activity and ask for help. Of course, you can and should silently pray for guidance yourself. You can also lead the class in prayer. Direct students to pause, put down all materials, and recite together a simple memorized prayer that all students know, such as the Our Father.

The second question is more complex. Repentance and forgiveness are fundamental to the Christian life, and so teachers (and parents) understandably want to teach children to apologize for misbehavior. The difficulty in the classroom is this: Apologies cannot be forced.

In certain cases it may be appropriate to require a student to write a note of apology. Consult with your DRE or pastor about whether a given situation warrants a written apology and whether the parish is in a position to require one. My criteria are that the matter is serious; the student knows the behavior was wrong; and the student is mature enough to have avoided the behavior. You cannot force the student to actually write the note, but you can require that the student not rejoin regular classroom activities until it is written.

Requesting an out-loud oral apology in front of the class is not a good idea. Doing so provides an opportunity for more misbehavior, such as silly or disrespectful fake apologies. It encourages a contest of wills and takes up time and attention that properly belong to classroom teaching. (Note that requiring an oral apology is often an appropriate strategy when used by parents at home. But for the reasons explained here, it is not a good choice in the classroom.)

However, a student may choose to apologize spontaneously. If so, accept the apology simply and graciously. "I forgive you," or "thank you for apologizing" is all that is necessary. If you are still miffed about the incident or you suspect the student is not truly sincere, keep your mouth closed! Juvenile comebacks, sarcasm, and supplementary berating are never appropriate in the classroom. If a student gives a disrespectful or fake apology, give it as little attention as possible and continue teaching.

You can discourage acting out by cultivating an attitude of disinterest as you matter-of-factly respond to misbehavior and quickly move on to better pursuits. Save your energy and enthusiasm for when you catch students behaving as they ought.

ELEMENT #6
Encourage Your Students!

It's not easy to be good all the time. We all need friendship, support, and help with motivation. You can encourage your students by creating incentives for good behavior, by building personal connections, and by outright cheerleading.

Should You Use an Incentive System?

There are any number of elaborate systems designed to reward good behavior in the classroom—colored cards, tokens, and points systems that allow students to earn prizes or awards. Used in isolation, these are not in themselves a system of discipline. All the elements of discipline need to be in place. But for some students and teachers, points-and-rewards systems can be one means of encouraging students. If you find a simple, manageable method that you and your colleagues personally enjoy using, and that your students respond to well, by all means use it.

A good approach to incentive-based encouragement does not need to be complicated, however, and does not have to include any extra system above and beyond normal classroom teaching. Let's look at the three components of a good set of incentives.

1. Immediate feedback. When students behave well, let them know. Simple verbal and physical cues, such as smiling, making eye contact, and saying, "That was a great answer," or, "Thank you for waiting so patiently" provide that feedback. If you put into place a formal incentive system, you can record points earned and lost on the blackboard or use a more durable system such as a star chart or the Pebble Jar described below.

2. Delayed rewards given during the same class period. At the end of class, or at the end of a segment of class, acknowledge and reward good behavior. Simple praise and kindness are essential and should never be overlooked. When planning your class, an easy way to build in a student-motivator is to put a fun activity at the end of class. The more students cooperate, the more time they have at the end of the period for the activity they love.

What do students love? Some catechists give out candy or prizes as rewards at every class, but this is not always a realistic or desirable option. Parents may be aggravated by the clutter and junk food, and the catechist's budget may not allow for so many treats. Children who are already overloaded with sweets and toys at home may not be especially motivated. Students themselves often long for more meaningful and personal motivators. For example, I've known students who get excited by music time, puppet shows, quiz games, open-ended discussion of their own concerns and problems, and, much to my surprise, meditative prayer. Young children do enjoy earning stickers and collecting other tangible proof of their good behavior—often something as simple as having a completed assignment to bring home to their parents.

3. Rewards earned over several weeks or a semester. Save big rewards for longer-term achievement. A zero-cost way to reward the whole class for completing a unit is by hosting a game day. Teach your lesson, but teach it via fun Bible- and religion-themed games. Another possible reward is a snack day, when students may bring in a snack to share with the class. (Tell parents about any restrictions due to allergies, chemical sensitivities, or choking hazards.) If you have the budget for prizes, you can distribute holy cards, bookmarks, medals, or other goodies at suitable intervals, after so many points have been earned, lessons completed, or Bible verses memorized.

If you plan long-term incentives for young children, create a way to visibly track their progress, such as a bar chart on the wall that is slowly colored in as they work toward the finish line. Catechists Dorian Speed and Elaine Bonacci both like to use the Pebble Jar for tracking progress toward behavioral goals. Pebbles (or marbles) are added to the jar when the teacher observes students behaving appropriately and may be removed when students misbehave. Ms. Speed cautions that removing marbles for misbehavior can backfire. "I am very opposed to punishing the group for the actions of a few because it reinforces their role as the bad apples in the room." Ms. Bonacci emphasizes that adding marbles must always be the teacher's unprompted choice, or students will learn to beg for marbles! When the jar is full, the class receives its earned reward.

Picking Incentives Your Students Love

How do you know whether your students will even care about a particular treat? Some students love music, others are indifferent.

Some students thrive on quiz games, others find them boring or intimidating. One year my fifth-graders begged at the end of every class session to be allowed to light the candles, put on the soft music, and pray. The next year, I had such a high-energy group that we never even attempted such a slow-and-reflective approach to prayer. What if you plan a particular reward, but it turns out to be punishment?

For summer and holiday programs, our curriculum is always heavy on fun stuff, so as long as I plan a game or craft for the second half of the lesson, we usually do fine. I pack a backup supply of coloring sheets and word games for students who are bored by the chosen activity.

The regular school year is more serious and has a strong academic focus. Running around the gym and playing ball for twenty minutes every class is not an option. I like to begin the semester with open eyes and ears. I watch my students to determine: What is their energy level? As we move through the class, what kinds of activities do they enjoy the most? What parts of the lesson are most difficult for them? If I have several choices in the back of my head for ways to end the class session, after observing the group for half an hour, I can make an educated guess about how to wrap up the class. Over the course of several weeks, we tweak the daily routine. If we seem to be struggling, I try to rotate into the mix some new types of learning activities that I think the students might enjoy. When we find one that everyone loves, I turn that one into the incentive.

The Personal Connection

There's nothing wrong with using formal incentives, but genuine encouragement is something much more personal. Students need to know that you care about them, that you are interested in who they are and what they have to say, and that you are genuinely glad to see them each week. Greet your students as they arrive, make eye contact, and smile. Look for moments when you can connect one-to-one. It can be a quick word of praise, a compliment, or a sincere question: "How are you?" "Did you have a good vacation?" "How's school coming so far?" "How's your family doing?"

Young or less mature students may need some cheerleading to make it through an entire class session. Your words of encouragement need to be clear, explicit, and conveyed with visible warmth and bright eyes. Acknowledge the student's effort: "I know it's hard to sit still. You are doing a good job." Provide reassurance that the end is in sight: "We need to finish one more page and then we can do our next activity." Thank students at the end of the activity or the end of the class: "You listened very well today. Your help makes the class so much more fun."

It is easy to lose patience with a restless or challenging student. But if a student is coming to your class week after week, trying his best to participate but frequently getting a little too excited or distracted? That's an invitation to make a friend.

The elements of discipline are, at their heart, six ways of putting yourself at your students' service. Your students need to know by the example you set, the course you create, and your commitment to a peaceful and joyful classroom that you are on their side, hoping for the best for them no matter what.

We've mentioned several times the importance of effective class planning in carrying out that commitment. Let's take a look now at "rhythm and routine," the two principles that are the foundation on which all plans are built.

3

CREATING A CLASS THAT WORKS: RHYTHM & ROUTINE

A well-planned class creates the environment students need in order to behave. Have you ever watched a mischievous toddler try to "make cake?" As in meal planning, it is not enough to toss all the ingredients on the table and hope for the best. Showing up to class with a list of ideas but no strategy invites the same sort of chaos—and indigestion! "Rhythm" and "routine" are the very basic structures of classroom planning. Use them to hold your lessons together and to prevent class-time collapse.

Rhythm: The Pace of Your Class

Rhythm is how your class feels: The ups and downs, quiets and louds, busy activities and calm moments. I use good rhythm to plan a class that flows naturally from one activity to the next. The pace should be comfortable, neither plodding and trudging, nor crammed, nor frenetic.

For each class, I want to choose a combination of activities that complement each other, like a well-balanced recipe. There should be times of intense learning and mastering skills, and times to relax and digest what we've learned. There should be time for younger children to move around, and for older students to share and discuss. There should be prayer. That prayer time should be long enough to allow the student to connect with God, but not so long that students grow restless and bored. I want to put my chosen activities into an order that builds from one step to the next and that wastes as little time and energy on transitions as possible.

It's easier to understand classroom rhythm if you can look at a few "sample menus." In a few moments we'll take a look at a class plan that uses rhythm effectively. But first let's see what routines are and why they matter.

Routine: The Engine That Keeps Your Class Moving

Routine means doing things the same way every time. We sometimes use the word "routine" to mean "dull" or "tiresome," but that's not what routines are for! Imagine if every time you went to the grocery store you had to figure out where the cash register had moved, what currency the store was accepting this week, and whether you needed to pre-pay or wait until checkout. You'd begin to wish for a little predictability, wouldn't you? We use routines all the time in daily life to make everything from getting dressed to driving to work run more smoothly.

The same is true in the classroom. Routines are tools that add power to your class:

○ Students are more confident because they know what they need to do and know that they are doing it well.
○ Time that would be spent giving detailed instructions can instead be spent on interesting lessons and activities.
○ Teachers can quickly answer noncourse-related questions such as, "Can I go to the bathroom?" without being distracted from the main lesson.
○ Moving from one activity to the next runs more smoothly because students know what they need to do and how to do it.

Routines take the guesswork out of the boring stuff so that all your energy and attention can be devoted to good teaching. There are two types of routines: The **overall routine** is a basic pattern for your class that you follow from week to week; **individual routines** are for specific tasks that either will definitely occur or that may be expected to pop up during class time.

The Overall Routine

The entire class can run on one overall routine that helps students anticipate what comes next. Activities will vary from week to week, but put the same general type of activities in the same order every week. An example for an early-years class might be:

Sample Routine

1. Coloring sheets, attendance
2. Opening prayer
3. Bible story
4. Discuss the Bible story
5. Bible craft
6. Cleanup
7. Closing prayer
8. Line up for dismissal.

Here's the overall routine we used for an evening vacation Bible school program:

Sample Routine

1. Students arrive in the main classroom, choose a coloring sheet or word puzzle to complete while waiting for class to begin.
2. Opening session: Prayer, music, introduction to the day's saint and virtue.
3. Walk to the Bible-story room for a live-action Bible story.
4. Walk to the craft room for an associated craft.
5. Return to the main classroom (since it is closest to the craft room) for instructions on the evening's game.
6. March downstairs to the gym for the running-around game.
7. Walk back upstairs to the main classroom.
8. Short discussion and Bible-verse practice time, then dismissal.

Following the same general pattern week after week helps your class run more smoothly. On weeks when there are changes in the routine, you can easily plan and communicate those changes. In the VBS routine above, we often had little hiccups in the evening. We used flexibility in the "main classroom" activities to extend or compress the class as needed. Students used the predictable cue of moving from room to room to tell them what type of activity was coming next.

Class Routines Build Suspense

We sometimes imagine "suspense" means "no idea what will happen next." But that's not true! A thriller isn't suspenseful because we walk into the theater with no idea whether there's going to be a fight with the bad guy, an afternoon of show tunes, or a dramatic reading of the Gettysburg Address. A movie is suspenseful when we know the bad guy has gotten into the house and we know the hero is going to have to fight him...but we don't know the exact details.

If students know that at the end of every night there is a short game, they are motivated to work quickly so there is as much time as possible for the game. If they know that the Bible story only lasts ten minutes, it is much easier to sit still at minute nine than if they have no idea how much longer the lesson is going to be.

You can intentionally add extra suspense to your class by giving hints or teasers at the beginning of class that won't get answered until later in the class period. ("We're going to read about a Bible hero who gets tossed into the sea—can you guess who it is?") But time your teaser carefully according to the temperament of your students so they aren't distracted from the lesson trying to solve a mystery. With younger children, giving a hint or clue right before snack time is a motivator to eat and clean up quickly in order to find out the answer.

Individual Routines

Routines are also important for individual tasks. Have a routine for every action! When students arrive, what is the routine? For my fifth-graders one year it was: *Come into class, say hello to the teacher, get your books and folder from the box in the back of the room, sit down, and start working on your journal assignment.*

What is the routine for bathroom breaks? Is there a hall pass? Should students raise their hands and make their request? Or should they quietly get up and go tell the classroom assistant? For older students, do they need to wait until a designated break time?

What is the routine for prayer? Do students stand and face the crucifix? Do they sit and open their prayer books? Do they gather at a prayer station? Do they need to pass out rosaries? If one of the teaching goals of the class is to practice a wide variety of types of prayer, maybe the routine is to clean up books and supplies, then return to seats and wait for instructions.

What is the routine for dismissal? What is the process for ensuring the right student goes home with the right family? With large groups of students, dismissal can be one of the most difficult parts of the class period. Work with your DRE or pastor to find ways to make it run as smoothly as possible.

Develop your routines or procedures before the start of class. You will need to set aside time to tell students what to expect, show them exactly what to do, and to practice. Remember that your procedures might be different than what students had to do last year or are expected to do in their other classes at school. Make written instructions and post them in the class. This serves as a reminder for both students and adult volunteers. Forgetting the routine is not misbehavior. The only "consequence" is to be reminded of the proper procedure.

Use routines for nonroutine events as well: *What is the routine if someone comes to class late? If an unexpected visitor interrupts class? If someone comes to the class in the middle of a prayer time?*

These are not complicated situations. But if you're in the middle of opening prayers, wouldn't it be less disruptive if the student waits by the door, or silently takes a seat, instead of shuffling around the class gathering books and sharpening his pencil? Let your students know what to do in advance so you don't have to interrupt your prayers or lesson in order to give instructions. For older students, you can put a sign on the door instructing students and visitors what to do if they arrive during prayers. For example, "If you arrive during prayer time, please come inside quietly and wait by the door." With younger students, it is helpful to station an assistant by the door to ferry students inside.

The more class activities can be turned into mini-routines, the easier it is to conduct your class. Any time you do a new or unique activity, students will need to be taught how to proceed. The fewer "training sessions" required, the easier it is to manage the classroom.

Prepare a Routine Response
to Common Student Emergencies

Real-life happens. Have a routine planned for how you will help the student who feels sick, the student who is upset, the student who has an embarrassing situation that needs adult attention or assistance. Usually the student will indicate the need very discreetly. If possible I excuse the student to go to the office or restroom and ask an adult volunteer to go along if the student needs assistance.

The remaining students may wonder, "What's wrong with her?" or, "Why did he leave class?" An honest answer that respects your student's privacy is: "She needed to speak to the DRE," or, "He needed to leave early tonight." Resume class with no further discussion.

Rhythm, Routine, and Learning Styles

Pay attention! That's the message of cognitive scientist Daniel Willingham, whose research confirms what your mother always knew: You won't learn anything if you aren't paying attention. But here's what I've seen over and again when attending catechist-formation classes: Different people pay attention in different ways.

When I'm the student, there are certain activities I dread. Small-group sharing times are at the top my list. Ditto for the moment when we all have to stand up, get in a circle, and do some physical activity that demonstrates the moral of the instructor's lesson. But you know what? There are always—always—one or two participants who finish the small-group activity by saying, "Wow! That really helped me understand what you were saying earlier! It all makes sense now!"

I have a child who learns by talking. I might tell her, "It's important to wear your seat belt so you don't get hurt if I have to stop the car suddenly." My daughter will think about this for a moment. And then, with no prompting from me, she will launch into a speech explaining seven different examples of what might happen if she didn't buckle her seat belt. Explaining—or talking through what she just heard—is her way of paying attention. It's her way of processing her thoughts and getting them firmly into her head.

For me, the pen is my attention-keeper. When I attend a lecture, I always bring my spiral notebook and a pile of pens. As the instructor presents, I take pages of notes. When there isn't something I need to note, I seem unable to put down the pen. On a recent conference call, I found myself, as usual, filling the margins of my notebook with geometric designs. I made myself stop—and suddenly I wasn't listening to the call anymore. My mind had begun to wander. I went back to doodling and went back to listening. It's the way I pay attention.

A teacher trying to reach both my daughter and me might use a fill-in-the-blank study guide to help me learn by writing, and discussion questions to help my daughter process her thoughts out loud. (I'll be the one drawing in the margins of the study guide while the others discuss.) As we'll see in the next chapter, using props, pretend, and learning games can help certain students better pay attention and understand the lesson.

How does classroom behavior fit into this picture? As an

adult, I have the patience and self control to politely endure the activities that don't appeal to me. I also have the freedom to enroll in courses that I know are a better fit for my interests. (Want to infuriate parents? Make them attend a long, boring, mandatory meeting as a requirement for sacramental preparation. Adults don't like being bored any more than children do.)

Younger children don't have the tuning-out power of teens and adults. Faced with a boring-to-them activity, they'll find other ways to entertain themselves. When your students begin to act out in class, consider whether you are spending too much time on a single style of activity. One of the goals of good class-time "rhythm and routine" is to incorporate a steady flow of different ways to pay attention and explore the topic.

As you look for ways to add variety to your teaching methods, ask yourself: Is there more than one way students could do this activity? When I open class with a Bible study, I allow students to work individually or in small groups. This lets the readers read, the writers make notes in their journals, and the talkers quietly discuss the Bible passage with each other. A student who struggles with reading can be paired with one who loves to read aloud.

Sample Class: What Do Rhythm and Routine Look Like in Real Life?

Feeling overwhelmed by the prospect of getting your class plans organized? At the end of the book, after we've looked at some more advanced teaching and planning strategies, we'll learn an easy step-by-step method for building a set of class plans from scratch. But right now let's walk through an all-purpose class plan that uses "rhythm and routine" effectively. This is a robust and well-worn blueprint for building a class, but it is not the only successful approach! If you are new to class planning, use these ideas as a starting point, but play around with your plans to find the best "routine and rhythm" for your class.

1. Opening Activity

If students arrive as a group, for example, coming from another gathering room elsewhere in the building or from their previous class, then the "opening activity" is to get into place so that class can start. When students trickle in over several minutes or longer, begin class with a task that will keep students busy while they wait for their peers.

What kind of activity? You will be taking attendance and dealing with last-minute disruptions, so students need to be able to work independently. Choose an activity that doesn't need to be entirely completed during class time, as some students will arrive late and have little time to work on this. Here are some ideas:

○ Provide a coloring sheet, word puzzle, or worksheet related to the day's lesson.
○ Prepare a simple craft students can work on by themselves.
○ Give older students journal assignments, a Bible study, or a self-selected reading assignment from the class library.
○ Stock open-ended educational games, such as the Friendly Defenders flash cards, that can be played for any amount of time.

Opening assignments should be specific. Not "study for your test," but rather: "Answer the review questions on page 47 of your blue textbook." Write it on the board. Instruct students to come to you for a second assignment from your folder of backup activities if they finish early. For young children, consider keeping a supply of picture books and quiet toys such as felt-board Bible characters and foam blocks. Trickle-in time can work as a music time if you have a designated song leader who is free to focus entirely on leading the music.

Remember that you will need to establish a routine for how students come into class and what they are expected to do. If you greet all your students at the door in one group, take a moment as they stand at the threshold to review what they will do when they enter the classroom. ("Take a book from the green shelf, then find a seat at one of the long tables and get ready to read.") If students trickle in, write the arrival routine on the board. Plan to walk each student through the arrival process for the first few class sessions.

2. Opening Prayers

When all students have arrived, open the class session with short, simple opening prayers. At the beginning of class, students have the most energy and attention and are ready to work. This prayer routine sets the tone for the class but allows you to move quickly into the lesson before attention starts to lag. Opening prayers might include:

○ Traditional standbys: the Glory Be, Hail Mary, and Our Father.
○ New or seasonal prayers students need to learn, such as the prayer to Saint Michael or an act of contrition.
○ A short devotional liturgy, such as the Angelus or a decade of the Chaplet of Divine Mercy.
○ Intercessions that repeat each class, such as prayers for the pastor, the sick, or a parish mission.
○ Students' prayer intentions, if you have an efficient process for gathering them, such as having students write their prayers requests on a list as they arrive for class.
○ A free-form prayer of your choice, thanking God for the day's class time and asking for guidance as you teach.

Don't try to include everything! Choose one or a few elements, and put together an opening liturgy that takes no more than about five minutes. Make your opening prayers shorter and more structured for younger students. It is fine—helpful even—to repeat the same prayers every class session. Do not worry about becoming "boring." It is tempting to vary prayers constantly, but for opening prayers, routine and structure help keep the class focused.

If you wish to teach a new type of prayer every week, introduce it during lesson time and then pray the new prayer as part of closing prayers. Likewise, I usually save longer or more reflective prayer times until the end of the class. Particular types of prayer that require significant time and attention, such as the rosary or the Stations of the Cross, are an exception. In these instances, you may want to introduce and explain the prayer briefly once the class has assembled, then make the praying of the prayer the bulk of your lesson time. We learn to pray by praying!

3. Jump Into the Lesson

Get to work while students are fresh. Now is the time to dig into serious material and make a strong impression. Anything students must know should be presented early in the class period and reviewed as you teach. When making your class plans, divide your plan into "essentials" and "extras." Give some thought to how you can teach the essentials in a way that students will understand and remember what they need to know. Use the extras to complement the essentials and fill out your lesson. If time runs short, you can cut one of the extras and be confident you've still taught what students absolutely must learn today.

How will you open your teaching time? Consider one of these activities to draw your students into the topic:

○ Read, tell, or perform the Bible story around which your lesson is built.

○ Ask a short-answer discussion question related to the topic, such as, "What are ways you show people you love them?"

○ Ask review questions that lead into the topic.

○ Use a teacher-led group activity to guide discussion, such as giving students a list of actions and having students decide which ones are "loving" and which ones are "unloving."

○ If students completed a lesson-related Bible reading or worksheet as they arrived in class, open the lesson by discussing and explaining the reading or by going over the answers to the worksheet.

○ Just start teaching. It isn't necessary to have showy gimmicks. Sometimes, "Open your book to page 168" really is the best way to get class going.

Look for the balance between a class that is too light and one that is too dense. You'll hold students' interest if you fill your lesson with new and demanding information. Even as we need to meditate on the basics of our faith ("Jesus loves me"—what's more important than that!), every year students should see those basics fleshed out with more detail. As your curriculum spirals through the essentials year after year, make sure your course offers enough new material so that longtime religious-ed students don't feel everything they'll ever learn was taught in kindergarten.

That said, don't cram too much material into a single class session. It can be tempting to race through piles of facts in a desperate effort to make sure students learn everything they'll ever need to know before they graduate. You'll end up exhausted and your students won't learn. Prioritize and pick just a few key lessons to pass on each class session. As you teach, take breaks for questions, short discussions, and review. Slowing down for review and discussion gives students time to digest the lesson, while asking and answering questions lets you know how well students understand the material.

Don't automatically dismiss all "off-topic" questions, as long as they are asked in earnest and relate in some way to the course. Use your judgment to decide how much time should be devoted to extraneous questions. If students are sincere in their questioning, they are probably asking about a topic that is important for them to understand. Often what seems like sidetracking ("If I'm in the army, can I shoot someone in battle?" asked by a child a decade away from military service) points toward a need to come to terms with concerns in the news or family life, or to develop an understanding of how moral thinking works.

4. Fun Stuff

If you have planned a craft or game, put it after your traditional lesson time. Younger students will be starting to get restless and are ready for a physical, hands-on learning activity. Older students don't need games and crafts, but if you include them, put them after the formal lesson. This prevents the dessert-before-dinner problem. All students benefit academically from fun quizzes or learning games that help them review and test their knowledge. Likewise, a service project such as making rosaries or sending notes to soldiers serving abroad can help teens connect with the Church as they practice the works of mercy.

Crafts

Let's look at a few tricks for preventing craft-time disasters. First of all, make the craft yourself ahead of time to work out any technical difficulties and so students can see an example of the final product. Consider whether students will pay attention to directions better if they don't yet have supplies in hand or if they need to have some of their materials in front of them so they can see up close what materials went into making your model. If the craft is complicated, it may be helpful to make a demo model for every table. For a multi-step process, you may need to have models in various stages of completion so students can easily see what the project should look like at each step.

How will you hand out supplies? Plan ahead to make an efficient, orderly process that both prevents a free-for-all and avoids long waits while a single teacher helps a dozen students one-by-one. If you need to put paint into paper cups or pompons and goggle-eyes into zipper bags, remember that you cannot be divvying out materials while also taking attendance, teaching, or supervising restroom breaks. Figure out a way to prepare the craft supplies before students arrive. If supplies such as glue or paint must be given out at the last minute, recruit extra help. Give your helpers clear directions before class begins so that you aren't training your volunteers while students wait.

Have a strategy for how to handle half-finished projects. Will students take home a selection of supplies in a zipper bag? What will they do with wet glue or wet paint? If the craft needs to dry, you can make it into the opening activity so that it can dry during the remainder of class. Parents do not want an open cup of tiny beads or a project covered in wet tempera paints to transport home at the end of class.

Games

Games pose some of the same challenges as crafts—but instead of trying to keep glitter glue off the crucifix, you're trying to keep freeze tag from turning into open combat. As with crafts, advance planning is the key to success. Test new game ideas on a handful of volunteers—perhaps your own children or a few recruits from the playground after Mass. If you create an obstacle course or other physical challenge, testing is absolutely necessary to ensure that the game is neither laughingly easy nor maddeningly difficult. If possible, set up your game before class begins. If that is not possible, walk through the setup process once or twice so that when it's time to start the game, you can easily direct volunteers and set up quickly.

Volunteers need clear instructions. If teens or other adults will help run the game, walk them through the game before class begins. Written instructions can be helpful. Be clear and firm about how the game will be played. Consider the maturity of your game leaders and give explicit instructions as needed, such as, "You may only tag students on the arm or shoulder," or, "do not get the same student 'out' more than once per session."

Plan ahead for crowd control as you introduce the game. Have students gather and sit down in a designated spot, or stand with feet firmly planted, while you give game instructions. Review the ground rules and remind students that those who cannot play respectfully will have to sit on the sidelines. Do not hand out balls or other equipment until you are ready for students to play. It may be helpful to have one student assist as you demonstrate how the game is played. Have students practice responding to necessary commands, such as stopping and starting play at the blow of the whistle.

Think about your ending strategy for your game, but use your judgment as the game progresses. If the game ends too quickly, do you want to play a second round or move on to a different activity? If the game gets out of control, call a halt. Decide whether a rule review or game modification is appropriate, or whether it is better to stop the game altogether. Children are marvelously creative in inventing games and may have good suggestions on how to modify the game. They will also be enthusiastic in recommending a favorite game from a previous class session. Follow their lead if it's a suitable choice.

The Return Trip From Planet Fun to Planet Class

It's easier to get children excited than it is to quiet them down. Whether you've put games and crafts toward the end of the class period (as this sample plan does) or there's more class work ahead, some children will be tempted to keep the party rolling. Plan to close high-energy activities with a short calming routine. After a craft, cleanup time can serve this purpose. Consider closing game time with a series of final movements that involve calmly and quietly transitioning back to regular classroom behavior. For example, lead a quick round of Simon Says: "Simon says reach for the sky, Simon says stand on your toes, Simon says tiptoe to your seats...."

5. Cleanup

Depending on your class-time activities, you may have little to no mess, or you may be able to clean as you work. Most of the time, though, you'll need to set aside about five minutes for cleanup time. Allow additional time the first time you teach students the cleanup routine and any time you have an especially messy activity. For more complicated cleanup processes, call a formal halt so you can give instructions. Have students stop all activity, put supplies or equipment down, and listen to you. Tell students that they are now moving back from fun time to work time. Provide clear, simple instructions on what students need to do:

We'll put our projects on the drying rack, put supplies in the yellow bins, and make sure all scrap paper is cleaned up off the floor.

Or:

We'll put balls in the red basket, orange cones in the card-board box, and then line up by the door to go upstairs.

Three-step instructions are easy to remember and repeat as you keep students on track. When students have finished cleaning up, you may need to provide a second set of instructions. For example, if the return to class is more complicated than simply sitting back down at their desks, you might say:

We're now going to walk back to our classroom. We are going to whisper in the hallway so we do not disturb other classes. We will hold the door open for the person behind us as we go up the stairwell. When we return to class, please sit down and get ready to pray.

6. Closing Prayers

It's easier to pray when the room is neat and clean. If time has gotten away from you, and you have to choose between a few quick prayers amid paper scraps or skipping prayer altogether, the call is yours. If you find that you are always running out of time for cleanup and prayers, reassess your class plans. You may be trying to cram too many activities into the class session. Pare back your lesson and set an alarm so you know to stop teaching and start cleanup while there is still time. At the start of every class session I write a quick outline of the course on the top corner of the board, with start times next to each activity. If the board says "7:10—Clean Up," I remember to stop teaching at 7:10.

What Kind of Closing Prayer?

In choosing your closing prayers, consider your goals for the class. Is prayer itself one of the primary elements of the course? If so, allow enough time for more elaborate prayer services, for student-led intercessory prayer, for meditative or reflective prayers, for saying a decade of the rosary, for listening to sacred music—whatever meets the goals of the course and the needs of your students. If memorizing certain prayers is one of the course objectives, repeat those prayers every class period until students know them by heart. Sometimes your religious-education course won't have prayer as a major focus. In that case, a quick blessing or prayer response, or simply bidding students farewell, is an acceptable alternative.

Consider also the rhythm of your class and whether your students will be ready for the type of prayer you'd like to include. Don't plan a reflective or meditative prayer session back-to-back with a craft or high-energy game. The focused, manual work of a craft uses up the same kind of energy needed for meditative prayer. Games will leave students too excited to be able to settle down for reflective silence. Instead, plan a short prayer service similar to opening prayers.

So What Is Meditative Prayer, Anyway?

First of all, be assured that meditative prayer is nothing weird or goofy. It is a quiet time to connect to God in a personal, private way. *Lectio divina* is meditative prayer on a passage of Scripture. The rosary is meditative prayer set to the backdrop of a chain of memorized prayers. Eucharistic adoration is meditative prayer in the company of the Blessed Sacrament. It all adds up to the one foundation of prayer: "Be still and know that I am God" (Psalm 46:11).

Here's an approach that works in the classroom:
Make a clean transition. Put away books and supplies and have students find a seat in a comfortable place where they have adequate personal space. You can choose to let students sit on the floor, but don't let that be an invitation for silliness. Don't dictate a

precise posture but instead offer one or two suggestions that may be helpful. For example, direct students by saying, "You may wish to fold your hands and put them in your lap, or to rest your head on the table so that you are completely relaxed."

Set the tone. Consider dimming the lights and lighting candles if possible. You may wish to play reflective music during this time, or you may prefer complete silence. Invite students to settle in for prayerful silent reflection. A student who is unable or unwilling to sit quietly during this time should be directed to do an alternative quiet activity (such as a coloring sheet or word puzzle) in the hallway with an assistant.

Choose the prayer focus. This can take many forms. There are guided meditations that you can read directly from a script or that you can develop. Students can meditate on a particular mystery of the rosary, on a Bible verse, or spend time with Jesus silently talking about a question or concern they have. You may read the words of a well-known prayer and invite students to reflect upon it or play a traditional hymn and invite students to listen to the words in a meditative manner.

The prayer focus will determine whether eyes should be opened (gazing at an icon or looking at words to a hymn) or closed (listening to the meditation, then silently communing with our Lord). If you plan to meditate on a particular prayer, hymn, or Bible passage, it is helpful if you have already studied it during class time. You don't want students wondering what a "trespasser" is when they are in the middle of reflecting on the Our Father word by word.

Allow silent prayer time. Encourage students to spend this time speaking with Jesus (silently) in their own way and listening in that same manner. Assure students there is no right or wrong way to spend this silent time in the presence of God.

Close the prayer session before students grow restless. It is better for students to pray too little and be hungry for more than to grow bored and begin to entertain themselves with distractions. You will want to plan the prayer session for a time that is free from interruptions. If it is possible students will be interrupted, let them know in advance what they should do if that interruption occurs. ("If the bell should ring while we are still praying, quietly conclude your time with Jesus and silently get up and go to the door.")

Give students a few minutes to "come out" of prayer time. Some students may wish to share what they experienced during prayer, but don't pry or push. Prayer is personal.

7. Time Filler

Is there extra time after closing prayers? Have a time-filler in your backup plans. Choose an activity that requires no props, supplies, or rearranging of furniture and that can be as long or as short as time permits. Here are some possible time-filler activities:

- ○ Practice a memory verse or prayer.
- ○ Quiz students on material already studied.
- ○ Open Q&A: Take questions on any religious-education topic. If you don't know the answer, write down the question and bring back the answer next week.
- ○ Play sit-in-place games such as Telephone, Twenty Questions, I Spy, Hangman, and Simon Says. You can put a religious-education twist on most of these by using names of saints, religious vocabulary, or parts of the church as your game topics. With Telephone, pre-screen students' choices to avoid gross-out humor and other inappropriate content. Don't try to play a religious-ed version of Simon Says. Just play it for fun.

Let the kids talk to you! This is a good time for a class discussion that refocuses on the lesson in a new way or opens next week's topic. You can invite students to share personal news and prayer requests for the class to keep in prayer over the coming week. Students might also enjoy discussing:

○ What they liked most about class.
○ Something fun they did in the past week.
○ Their favorite part of Mass.
○ Their favorite devotion, prayer, or sacramental.
○ A favorite saint.
○ Something interesting that will be happening soon.
○ What they have planned for an upcoming holiday.
○ A good joke they heard.

Some students will enjoy chatting, others prefer to listen. Either is fine.

What if you need a time-filler every week?

If you are consistently finishing class ahead of schedule, you have room for more material. You can add time to one of the earlier sections of your class or you can turn one of the "time fillers" into a regularly scheduled learning activity. Experiment until you find an activity that meets a student need or that students happen to love.

8. Dismissal

Dismissal should be an organized, pre-planned process. Find out in advance:

- How will you, the teacher, know when it is time for dismissal?
- When will you give back student cell phones if they were taken up during class time?
- Where will parents pick students up?
- How will students get to that rendezvous point?
- Who will stay with students until parents arrive?
- What are students supposed to do while waiting for their parents?
- What do you do if a student's parents are late?

Use this information to develop instructions for your students. If you are in charge of your students' dismissal, teach them what you expect right from the start. The effort you put into building good routines at the start of the school year will pay off over the months ahead. When everyone knows what to do and how to do it, tempers stay cooler, students respond more attentively, and everyone has more fun in class.

The sample class routine we've just explored is only one of many ways to organize class time. It is a durable pattern, but often you'll need to come up with a unique plan custom-made for your class. In the chapters ahead, we'll look at some of the common challenges teachers face that can undermine classroom discipline and learn some techniques for preventing and responding to problems. Reviewing these techniques will help you choose appropriate activities for your students. We'll finish in chapter 8 by learning how to assemble all your ideas into a set of personalized class plans. Let's start our problem-solving with a look at the group of students most infamous for overwhelming catechists with their energetic antics: the very young.

4

TURNING THE YOUNG AND THE RESTLESS INTO THE ATTENTIVE AND INSTRUCTED

Young children are hungry to learn about Jesus and to know him personally. They are not hungry to sit like statues and endure long hours of lecturing. You can prevent discipline problems by teaching classes that build on the natural needs and desires of young children. Let's look at five characteristics of young children and see how you can use them to create joyful, fun-filled ways to pass on the faith.

#1

Kids Need Active Love

Befriend your students from the very start. Building attentive friendships with students encourages them to pay attention in class. They know there is another smile or kind comment waiting for them from the same place the first dose came from. Children fear favoritism, so be aware of your interactions with each student and actively work toward giving each child the attention and consideration he or she deserves. The flip side of friendship is the cost of losing it. When students feel your affection for them, they feel the pain of disappointing much more keenly. Very mild censure is often all that is needed to refocus a student who genuinely wants to please you.

How do you make friends with your students? Some of the best early-grades teachers are masters of The Teacher Wink. It's a flash of the eye that lets the recipient know he isn't forgotten and will get his turn soon. I can't wink (I look like I have a gnat in my eye), but I'm pretty reliable for a smile or an exchanged glance. Build rapport by remembering and using names, by keeping track of who plays what sport, or complimenting students on an interesting hairstyle or outfit. A sincere, "How are you?" followed by genuine interest in the student's answer, speaks volumes. However you do it, it all adds up to, "I'm glad you're here."

These are not fake attentions. Rather, you are making an effort to outwardly show the goodwill toward your students that is within you. The attention you give your students should flow from an inherent respect for their human dignity, without any ulterior motive. Friendship is a gift, not a bargain. Likewise, classroom friendship between student and teacher should respect the firm boundaries appropriate to the teacher-student relationship.

#2

Kids Love to Talk

If adults enjoy a class or a lecture, they will participate spontaneously—asking questions, sharing experiences, laughing out loud at your jokes. Children sit silently when they are absorbed by the lesson; they chitchat and interrupt when they are bored. Just like adults, though, kids do want a chance to share and interact. Small children thrive on structured talking times built into the class. We'll look at three aspects of talking time here and see a few more in just a moment.

Use Short-Answer Sharing Times
to Let Everyone Have a Turn Talking

Young children want to share everything they know. They want to tell you about their day, about their favorite flavor of ice cream, and about their one-eyed stuffed dog. And anything else you'll give them time to say. I like to start lessons with a short-answer question related to the day's topic. For example, if we are talking about how God takes care of us, I might ask, "Does anybody here have a mom or dad or someone else in your family who does something to take care of you?"

Of course every student has some such person. So they all take turns answering, usually in a predictable pattern: "My mom makes me dinner." "My dad makes me dinner." "My favorite food is cheeseburgers." "I was at McDonald's and I saw a guy with green hair." "My favorite color is purple." "My favorite is blue...."

You will have to direct your students back to the topic with frequent, "Who else has another way someone takes care of you?" reminders. But the kids love sharing about themselves, the discussion provides a natural topic-opener, and it only takes a few minutes. Use these short-answer questions throughout the class to keep kids awake and engaged.

No One Gets Called Upon
Who Is Not Sitting Quietly and Still

You asked the students, "Who has a pet that you help take care of?" and now two dozen seven-year-olds are falling out of their seats, moaning and squeaking and waving hands wildly, desperate to tell you that they, too, have a cat, but it isn't named Oreo because Oreo died last year, and they got a new cat named Snowball who drinks from the birdbath. Only you'll never hear it over all the grunting and begging, and someone's about to get an eye poked out in the competition to get called on first.

Tell the kids this: "I have a rule in my class: I don't call on anyone who is not sitting quietly."

Then keep your rule. The first time you say to a student, "I'm sorry, I would like to hear what you have to say, but you are not being quiet so I am not allowed to call on you," the rest of the class will get a powerful message:

Being Quiet = Getting the Attention I Want

Use this rule in everything you do. Then when Miss Wavy and Mr. Groaner do quiet down, call on them with great relish: "Thank you so much for sitting quietly and still. I can't wait to hear what you have to say."

Ask "Shout-Out" Questions to Reinforce the Lesson

A stadium full of fifty-year-old men can be entertained by having them all shout out the name of their favorite football team in unison. A classroom full of seven-year-olds is no different.

"Which angel came to tell Mary she was going to be the mother of Jesus?"

"Gabriel!"

"I can't hear you. Who?!"

"GABRIEL!!"

"And did Mary say 'yes' or 'no?'"

You can pep-rally any one-word answer you like. Note that it is easier to shout the sacrament of *"confession!"* than *"reconciliation!"* Practice your shout-outs at home to yourself so that you make sure you are prompting the kids for a suitably shout-able word.

Kids Want to Learn Adult Stuff

If I were to name the single most common mistake in religious-education programs, it would be watered-down curricula. Children do need lessons that are compact and clearly communicated. R-rated Bible stories and saints' lives need to be edited for a young audience. Topics should be approached with the child's limited experience and maturity in mind. Certainly classes cannot move at the speed of an adult course because children lack the background knowledge of adults. But children are capable of learning far more than we sometimes realize.

So we take fewer stories and study them well. We take time to learn the big words. We get to the heart of the story, see how the details play out, and then back up and compare them to our own lives. If the student book contains only a very short, easy-reader summary of the topic you are teaching, that does not mean you teach at that level. You are the adult. Research the details of your topic, then choose how to present a lesson that expands on the simple summary in the student book. Let's look at some ways to beef up a flimsy lesson and catch the attention of young thinkers.

Teach Difficult Vocabulary Words

Small children like big words. It's fun learning to carefully pronounce words like "Mesopotamia" and "Annunciation." Say the word slowly and clearly for the class. Have them repeat it one syllable at a time:

"Mess." *"Mess!"*
"Oh." *"Oh!"*
"Mess. Oh." *"Mess Oh!"*
"Po." *"Po!"*

"Mess. Oh. Po." ....Eventually you get to *"Mess. Oh. Po. Tay. Mee. Uh!"*

And then a little faster, and a tiny bit faster, and then keep it there. Don't say it too fast. Let each child practice saying it aloud alone, loud and clear. Congratulate them. Little kids love getting to show off a word like "Mesopotamia."

And of course give your students the definition or context. "Abraham came from Ur in Mess-Oh-Po-Tay-Mee-Uh." (A star on a laminated map is helpful here.)

Then you quiz: "Where did Abraham come from?" Kids take turns answering: *"Ur in Mesopotamia!"*

And then, "Who came from Ur in Mesopotamia?" *"Abraham!"*

It isn't an enormous amount of content. Small children can only learn so much in one class session. But boy is it fun, and it lays the groundwork for later study.

Memorize in Threes

Organize your lesson to teach about a set of three. Emphasize the set, and make a short definition or explanation to go with each word.

Father, Son, Holy Spirit.
Deacon, Priest, Bishop.
Grave matter, full knowledge, freely chosen.
Abraham, Isaac, Jacob.

Throughout the class period, have the kids chant the set of three out loud as a group. Then they can take turns volunteering to say the set one by one. This should be fun—you should be happy about what they are learning, and they should have a sense you are pleased with their ability to learn. Use your short definition or explanation to create out-loud oral quizzes. Be excited! It's a giant pep rally in which students get to shout back the name of the winning word.

Some questions can be answered with the whole set of three, such as, "Who are the Trinity?" and "What are the three conditions for mortal sin?" Other questions ask the children to identify which of the three matches the definition: "Who is the father of Isaac?" "Which member of the clergy is in charge of a diocese?"

Play "Three Clues" to Review Vocabulary

Take the definitions the kids have learned and use them to create a guessing game. You call out up to three clues. Kids can shout out the answer as soon as they guess. Read all three clues and have the whole class shout the answer, even if someone knew the answer before all the clues were given.

> *"He traveled from his homeland of Ur in Mesopotamia to the Promised Land."*
> *"He was married to Sarah."*
> *"His son was Isaac."*

By the third clue, kids should be shouting out *"Abraham!"* Take a look at how this next set of clues helps teach several lessons in one:

> *"He is one of the three persons of the Trinity."*
> *"The Bible says he is the Word of God."*
> *"He became man and was born of the Virgin Mary."*

At clue #1, kids are throwing out guesses from their set of three they learned earlier. Clue #2 is an important teaching point every Catholic needs to master. Clue #3 is the ringer that gives away the answer and sheds light on the earlier statements.

Remember that small children love repetition. They'll be happy to shout away at the same quiz questions week after week because they take satisfaction in being able complete the puzzle over and over again.

Say Things Opposite.
Use Silly Questions to Lure Kids Into Leaping at the Truth

All humor hinges on a comparison. Among grown adults, the comparisons can be very sophisticated...A Jesuit, a Dominican, and a Cistercian are stranded on a deserted island....

Young children delight in games of opposites:

You say: "Jesus wanted to talk to God the Father, so he got out his cell phone, right?"

Kids shout: *"Nooo!"*

"Then how did he talk to God the Father?"

"He PRAYED!"

"Oh, right. He prayed...."

Any lesson point can be introduced via silly statements and opposites. "Mary and Joseph had to travel to Bethlehem, so first they went on the Internet and ordered plane tickets...." "Saint Martin of Tours saw the poor man, but he just kept on riding, right?" "Saint Clare's parents didn't want her to follow her religious vocation, so she stayed home and got married, right?"

Sometimes students will know the correct answer; sometimes you will need to lead them down that path. "How did people travel in the time of Jesus?" "Was Joseph very rich, and did he have a team of horses to pull a magnificent wagon?"

This method is fun, but more importantly, it lets students come to conclusions on their own. It makes learning more active and more personal, and it increases the likelihood they will remember the lesson.

4

Kids Have Powerful Imaginations

Adults demand elaborate costumes and films shot on location. Kids crown King Arthur with a scrap of aluminum foil and joust with drinking straws. Take advantage of this childhood superpower by activating your students' imaginations.

Use props

Did you know that in his youth, Saint Martin de Porres trained to be a barber-surgeon? It was training that would shape his vocation to come. When presenting the life of Saint Martin to a group of young students, we used three props: A pair of scissors, a stethoscope, and a stuffed cat. "Barber-surgeon" is a strange word that doesn't make sense to modern ears. Seeing a teen pretend to cut hair and listen to heartbeats illustrated the profession more clearly than any long explanation of the history of medicine could have done. What about the cat? Among his many charitable works, Saint Martin founded a veterinary hospital!

Using props helps students see what is hard to explain. It is also a way to engage students' curiosity. What are they going to do with those scissors? Why is there a cat here tonight? Pulling out a prop poses a question in the student's head for which your lesson has the answer.

Pretend

One summer in vacation Bible school, our class was pretending to be sharing a meal together as the early Christians might have done. We had fake food—bread and grapes—some plates, an empty pitcher, and cupped hands for glasses. The kids happily spent five minutes pretending to serve and eat it all. One kindergartner spied a basket of rubber bracelets (related to another activity) in the corner of the room. She fetched the basket and announced, "Who wants spaghetti?"

Games of pretend can be elaborate. For special events, you can build background sets and invite the kids to re-create an entire Bible story. But they can also be short and easy. Spend two minutes scouring the room and herding pairs of imaginary animals onto an invisible ark. (Put up your invisible umbrellas when the "rain" starts.) Throw an invisible net over the side of the invisible fishing boat at your desk, then call more and more students to come help you pull it up, because it is miraculously so full of fish. Travel from slavery in Ireland (over by the chalkboard) with Saint Patrick, all the way around your classroom, onto a boat, and into freedom in Gaul.

Games of pretend are the way children explore ideas. Acting out the details of a story helps students remember the details. Engaging the imagination via games of pretend while studying Scripture is the precursor to *lectio divina* in years to come.

Have Volunteers Help Act Out the Day's Lesson

I love my DRE because she appreciates a good foam sword as much as I do. For Saint Joan of Arc, we assigned four teens to play the roles of Saint Joan, the French general, the dauphin, and the English general. The kids watched as the teens pantomimed, while I narrated the opening of the story.

Then we recruited an army. Eight young volunteers were issued soft foam swords and got to act out the battles between the English and the French. We had just two: One battle where the French "won," which represented all the successful missions Saint Joan led. We paused to crown the dauphin after the recapture of Orleans. The second battle represented Joan's final battle in which she was captured by the English. Then the young recruits sat down and the teens finished our tale.

Every Bible story and saint's life has something that can be acted out by one or more volunteers. Often you can call up a student to serve as a prop for your lesson—have a student demonstrate how to properly receive Communion or play the role of the priest when teaching about confession. Pulling students into the lesson adds liveliness and suspense—what will the teacher make them do?—and provides a chance for active students to make good use of their willingness to perform.

#5

Kids Love Games

There is a time and a place for Christian children to get together and just play for the sole purpose of making friends and enjoying themselves in a safe, respectful environment. This is one of the goals of our vacation and holiday programs. Within the regular religious-education program, however, games need to *work*.

Fun? Yes. But they also need to reinforce the lesson in some way. Use true learning games liberally, and mostly-just-fun games sparingly. It is the balance between brightly colored vegetables with a tasty dip versus chocolate pudding for dessert. Prepare appealing meals but make them nutritious. Dessert should stand out as a treat.

We've mentioned in previous chapters the possibility of adapting games like Hangman or I Spy to religious education. Let's look here at more physically active games that can be used in an early-grades lesson. The game ideas below are just a start. They may not be a fit for your class, so always have a backup plan in case a game flops. There are a number of books devoted to learning game ideas for all ages. Your DRE may have some on hand that you can consult for inspiration.

Lead Lesson-Related,
Teacher-Directed Physical Activities

Young children are made for movement. They need quantity time spent doing physical activities. Unfortunately, students may come to class straight from a long day of sitting still. Lesson-related, teacher-directed games are a way to meet the need to move without sacrificing the lesson.

Here are some ways to do this:

○ Assign students a set of physical actions that relate to the Bible story and have them perform that action on cue. For example, march in place every time you mention the Isrealites marching through the Red Sea or the desert wilderness.

○ Play review games using physical actions for the answer, such as, "If I say something true, hop on one foot and wave your hands; if I say something false, cover your ears and shake your head no."

○ Practice physical prayer and worship skills such as making the Sign of the Cross, genuflecting, and bowing to the altar with attention and precision. Any child who can study dance, karate, or skateboarding can learn "the moves" for church just as well.

○ Lead energetic sing-alongs such as "Joshua Fought the Battle of Jericho" and "Rise and Shine." If students find the Bible-school classics to be predictable and boring, add in surprising variations and invite students to invent their own improvements. (More than likely the oldies-but-goodies will seem like a novel invention to a generation raised on games played only with thumbs and music made by devices instead of voices.)

You may need to plan some "get the energy out" activities that serve no other purpose than to calm your class. Pause class and have students stand up and do jumping jacks or dance to music. You can set up a game in which students move when the music goes on and stand perfectly still when the music stops so that students are rewarded for practicing self control and following instructions. If you have the staff and the space, extra-active students can traipse off to the gym to run laps while the quiet ones color peacefully back in the classroom.

Use Games of Skill to Reinforce Ideas From Class

Games of skill provide an outlet for student energy but also require focus and concentration. If they are appropriately difficult—not too hard, not too easy—they give students a satisfying sense of accomplishment. Almost any game can be loosely tied to a Bible story, saint's life, or catechism lesson. Here are some games we've used at our parish:

○ Toss coins into a shoe after learning about Saint Nicholas.
○ Kick a ball through a minefield of orange cones without hitting any, just as students try to avoid situations and people that get them into trouble and sin.
○ Run an obstacle course in which teammates have to clean up after each other, just as in real life we have to forgive one another and help one another.
○ Shoot foam arrows at a target, a reminder of Saint Paul's admonition to "aim for the high mark."

These games are not a lesson in themselves. Some students will find the physical action helps them internalize the day's teaching. Reaching these "physical learners" is the primary goal of action games.

Some portion of your students, however, will not remember

the moral of the game; they'll just enjoy the game because it was fun. As long as the game is not taking up an undue amount of class time, that's fine. Consult with your DRE or pastor to determine how much game time is appropriate for a given class. Our parish saves running-around games for special events and for very young students. Older students generally don't need the physical outlet younger children do, so their time during a regular religious-education class may be better spent on more rigorous learning activities. But a dose of fun stuff is a nice way to make the observance of a feast day much more festive.

We've seen in this section some ways to work with the very young. Now let's turn to a problem more typical of older students: Keeping religious-ed veterans awake and interested without bewildering the newcomers who are just discovering the basics of the faith.

5

TEACHING BEGINNING AND ADVANCED STUDENTS IN THE SAME CLASS

B oredom is the enemy of good behavior. Teaching an interesting, substantial lesson is the solution. But how do you do that, when some of your students are very knowledgeable of the faith and others are just coming to religious-education classes for the first time?

If you are the lucky catechist tasked with the job of teaching a one-size-fits-all class, don't despair! By planning carefully, you can teach and review the basics, entertain the whole class with new and interesting details about the faith, and give all students fodder for reflection and personal growth. Here is a simple, three-part technique for teaching a single catechism class at multiple levels.

PART 1

Essentials

Pick the essential, entry-level memory items that students need to master. Make a list: the Trinity, the sacraments, the elements of the Creed, important prayers to memorize. Spend a small portion of each class period explaining, memorizing, and reviewing these items. Make it ten or twenty minutes at the very most, interspersed throughout the class period. Use a clear verbal cue to let new students know when you're covering the basics and to let more advanced students know that you're aware they've already seen this information before. Try, "We're going to go over some faith basics that are important for everyone to understand. There are no dumb questions! I want to make sure everyone understands these items on your handout. A few of you have seen these before, and if that's you, I want to make sure you've got your definitions down precisely and your vocabulary memorized."

In addition to these basics, include in your core lecture any items that are going to appear on a formal test. Provide repeated review of the information students will need to correctly answer test questions. (If there is considerable information on the test above and beyond "Catholicism 101," you will need to spend more time on this element of the class.)

Let students know that it's OK if they don't understand or remember everything that is said in class but that they need to master these few key pieces of information. Provide handouts, worksheets, and study guides that focus on just the essentials.

With older students, if time permits you can fill out your basics with more advanced explanations. For example, the study guide might offer a simple definition of the Incarnation. Your beginner students should focus on just this. Then take a moment to say something like, "And now I'm going to add some details that you don't need to memorize but that might be interesting." And then perhaps you share a bit about the historic debates that led to the formulation of the Nicene Creed.

Finish your aside by reemphasizing that students don't need to memorize all that history. Point back to the basics and assure all students that they only need to master the few points highlighted on the study guide. The extra information provides something for the advanced students to chew on when the study guide is otherwise 100 percent review for them.

In deciding whether to use the group lecture approach, gauge the extent to which your various students know the material. An alternative approach for the faith basics lesson is to divide the class into two or more groups. Advanced students can work quietly on an independent Bible study or group project while you meet with newcomers to go over introductory material. There might be a third in-between group who works on an assignment that reviews the material they don't know as well as they should.

PART 2

Heritage and History

Complement the basics with Bible stories, lives of saints, and devotionals. Students don't need to memorize these! Make them rich. Research the stories yourself so you can tell them with vivid details. While you may decide to include the better-known saints, Scriptures, and prayers, also pull out some lesser-known ones that your advanced students are unlikely to already know. This part of the class should be like watching a good movie—full of exciting detail but mentally reviving and relaxing.

A way to think about it: You are introducing your students to their faith family. These are the people and the stories and the traditions of their spiritual heritage. We do not introduce our children to their heritage by making them memorize the birth dates of every second cousin or sit in an empty room drilling facts about the history of Thanksgiving. We teach our children their heritage by telling the story of how Grandpa met Grandma; we introduce family traditions by attending Thanksgiving dinner or letting the kids help prepare the cranberry sauce. In the same way, this portion of the class lets all students relax and "meet the family" of our Catholic faith.

PART 3

Personal Growth

The demands of the Christian life are always fresh. We might have learned the Ten Commandments and the Great Commandment as small children, but a six-year-old and a sixteen-year-old apply these in very different ways. Whether your student is brand-new to the faith or has been practicing it for a decade, there is always a need to be pushed to take the Christian life to the next level.

You might wonder how "mature" kids are these days or what kinds of difficulties students face that you yourself never encountered. Just ask! Toss out an open-ended question, such as, "What are some things that kids your age are tempted to lie about?" Then listen. Invite students to brainstorm ways to avoid those temptations or to share stories of people they know who set the right example. Older students may enjoy discussing ways that their lives and their difficulties are different now compared to when they were younger.

Making the Most of the Three-Part System

By combining all three parts as three "layers" of your class, you can build a class that helps all students. These are not merely two separate classes run in parallel. Beginner students are explicitly taught the basics of the faith in a modest dose each week. More advanced students get a brief review but are presented with enough new material and demanding pastoral advice to give them something to ponder every class session. For the beginner, the "extras" are a way to get a taste of how the fundamentals are applied. For the advanced student, reviewing the basics in the context of new stories sheds light on the lessons they first learned years ago.

No matter what, be sure that you answer the most funda-mental question of evangelism: "What must I do to be saved?"

It is astonishingly easy to lose track of this one truth in the course of teaching all the other details of the faith. Make it your goal to present the Gospel anew every class. Just a sentence or two is all it takes. Students will surprise you with their questions as they try to figure out how salvation applies to them today. Come to your class with the heart of an evangelist and the rest will fall into place.

The "All I Need to Know About Jesus" Trap

Have you ever had a profound, heart-moving moment with God? A moment of clarity, when suddenly all the noise and details of everyday faith life seemed to lift away and you were touched by the utter simplicity of the Gospel? You realized in one moment that God's love alone is sufficient. Or that all your worries about some difficult decision could be set aside because the one thing that mattered was trusting in God's grace and provision. Or perhaps you had long misunderstood some aspect of our faith and suddenly you realized you'd been distracted by too many details, and a few words of redirection put you back on solid ground.

Resist the urge to make these "Aha!" spiritual moments the complete content of your class.

Yes, it is true, love alone suffices. God alone provides. Give your heart to Jesus and all else will follow. These important truths make a powerful refrain for your teaching. But your religious-education class cannot be a one-hour meditation on a single idea. Students' minds do not work this way. Instead, pick out your key idea—perhaps for the sacrament of reconciliation you want to focus on God's mercy or on the idea of turning your heart back to Jesus—and use that key idea as the theme around which you explore all the details.

Return to the refrain throughout the class period, but fill it in with verses. In our reconciliation class, "verse one" might lay the groundwork for why we have the sacrament; "verse two" might explain the mechanics of the sacrament, with a chance to practice going to confession with a partner; "verse three" might tell the story of a saintly priest who listened to confessions at all hours of the day and night, showing how important this sacrament is to the lives of the faithful. In between, come back to those one or two words—"mercy" or "repentance" or whatever it is that for you expresses the heart of the sacrament.

There's no single answer here—trust that God has placed you in this class today because he wants you to share your personal connection to the faith. Students need to meet other Catholics, to be encouraged in different ways by different teachers. In the next chapter we'll look at five situations in which students can feel disconnected from the faith community. As the catechist, you may wonder how to include certain students. Let's see how you can respond gracefully to every student who passes through your door.

6

BUILDING A CLASS THAT
INCLUDES EVERY STUDENT

Some students face tremendous struggles in their personal lives. How do I respond when a student's situation interferes with his or her ability to participate in class? As a catechist, it isn't my role to "diagnose" or "fix" my student. My job is to welcome every student and find ways to include each one in the class as best I can.

In this chapter we'll take a quick look at the highlights of five situations that are likely to occur at some point in your time as a catechist. You will no doubt encounter other somewhat different difficulties, so take the general principles here and adapt them as needed and appropriate. Two of the situations we'll explore involve unusual or difficult student behavior; the others are largely matters of choosing a well-built, flexible curriculum and being sensitive to students' needs. The focus of this chapter is on the number one, fundamental factor that controls the success of your class as a catechist and the one thing you can in fact control: your own behavior.

The Unresponsive Student

This student comes to class in body but remains entirely enclosed in an unresponsive shell. He may sit without moving at all, refrain from speaking, and refuse eye contact. He may show intense emotion, such as silently crying or shaking, or he may show no emotion at all.

Causes: You often can't know. The student may be struggling with a family conflict or an emotionally draining situation. The student may have been made to come to class against his will. Or the student may have a behavioral difficulty of some kind, and this is how he responds to the pressure of being in your classroom today.

Remember that children often don't have a choice about attending class. You and I, adults that we are, usually get to choose our activities. If we dread the thought of public speaking or group activities, we choose a different hobby that builds on our strengths. If we have a planned commitment and some sudden crisis leaves us emotionally drained and unable to participate, we can often excuse ourselves for the day. And when we do have to endure some unpleasant social chore, we have the experience and emotional maturity to put on our best face and plow through it. Children don't have these choices and resources.

Your response: Usually this student is not disruptive, so there's nothing you need to do immediately, other than to be kind and to offer a normal, friendly greeting. (Don't worry if he or she doesn't respond. Wait and see.) Teach your class as planned, and if the student does not eventually warm up and participate, don't try to force it.

Sometimes this student can be helped to participate in activities by having your gentle and respectful one-on-one attention. If so, that's great. But that will not always be the case. Pay attention and use your judgment. When in doubt, don't push.

If it is time for students to move from their seats to another place, invite the nonresponsive student to choose whether he wishes to move with the class or stay where he is. Have an assistant available to stay in the classroom if the rest of the class is moving to a different room. Let your student know that whatever he chooses is fine.

Take advantage of a time when the other students are working independently to go speak to your student. Let him know these things:

○ "I am glad you came to my class today."
○ "I am always happy to have you here."
○ "You do not have to do anything that makes you feel uncomfortable."
○ "God loves you, and you are important to him."

What if I Suspect a Child Is Being Abused?

Withdrawn or highly emotional behavior is not always a sign of a serious problem, but it certainly can be. In many states, catechists are "mandatory reporters." That means that if you believe a child is being abused, you are required by law to report your suspicions to the police. Regardless of the local law, we all have a sacred obligation to take steps to protect children from abusive situations. It is never acceptable to knowingly abandon a child in an abusive environment. Learn more about child-abuse prevention and reporting at virtus.org.

The Student Caught in a Religious War

This student has a Catholic parent or grandparent, but another close relative is strongly opposed to the teachings of the Church. The student may have been told that it is wrong to pray to saints, to say a "Hail Mary," or to use sacramentals and visual aids to prayer. Well-meaning friends or family may have said that Catholicism is a form of pagan devil worship. Or she may have been told that Christianity is nothing but a bunch of superstitions and fables.

If you are aware that your student is being pushed and pulled in this way, let her know these things:

- ○ "I'm glad you came to class today."
- ○ "It is my job to teach the Catholic faith, but it is not my job to force anybody to be Catholic. I respect you and care for you no matter what."
- ○ "I don't want you to do anything that makes you uncomfortable. Participate as much as you like, but I will not be angry or upset if there is something you'd rather not do today."
- ○ "If you have any questions about what Catholics do or believe, I am happy to answer them as best I can. It does not upset me if someone has an honest question."

During class time, be sensitive and respectful of how you speak of other faiths, whether you are aware of a mixed-faith family or not. That **does not** mean you teach that "all religions are basically the same," or that "it doesn't matter what you believe." **It means that you show respect for all people** and recognize that not everyone accepts the Catholic faith, even though they may be honest and earnest in their desire to know and serve God.

The Student With Significant Behavioral Difficulties

This isn't the class clown or the fidgety talker. This is the student who struggles with basic age-appropriate behaviors, likely due to a serious underlying problem. He may be disruptive, restless, or unable to follow simple social norms. Behavior disorders can be frustrating, but it is well worth the effort to accommodate the struggling student in your regular classroom and in the parish community. Here's what you need to know:

Everyone else knows about the problem already.
The parents know. The student himself knows. The other students know. No one is under any illusion that this child just needs to

"get with it" or "pull himself together." It isn't a lack of discipline that is causing his problems.

As a result, it is OK to make special accommodations for this child. Give him jobs or roles in the class that take advantage of his strengths and shield him from his weaknesses. Excuse him from activities that are too overwhelming for him. Have an assistant work with him one-on-one when needed.

Look for ways to modify your class so he can participate as fully as possible.
Communicate expectations with clear, explicit cues. Simplify activities to match your student's capacity for self control and direction-following. You may need to set up noncompetitive games, even at an age when other students are comfortable with games that have definite winners and losers. Be sensitive to situations that are overwhelming to your student, such as loud noises or a chaotic environment.

Your student may not have the same sense of physical limits as other children.
His "tag" might come out more like a "shove," or conversely, he may be hypersensitive to normal touch. He may have difficulty settling down after games that are exciting and highly active. Avoid putting your student in a situation where he will have to call on behavioral skills he simply does not yet have.

Your student may not be able to stay in class the entire class period.
He may have very little patience for boredom or be unable to cope with classroom assignments that are beyond his ability. The class may last too long for him. An assistant can provide an alternate activity outside the classroom for part of the class period.

Make a point of telling your student that you are glad he came to class.

Students with limited behavioral skills need clear communication. Don't rely on nonverbal cues alone. Say it out loud and explicitly: "John, I am so happy to see you today"; "Maria, I am glad you could come to class tonight."

Maturity and self control are traits that range across a spectrum. Clear communication, appropriate lessons, and actively managing the social atmosphere within the class can benefit all students. As Christian leaders, it is absolutely essential that we lend our support to the student who "doesn't fit in." **There should be no tolerance of mockery, teasing, bullying, or rudeness from any quarter.**

The Student Who Is Behind the Class Academically

This student is grouped with her age group, even though she is unable to work at the same academic level as the other students. She may have an obvious cognitive disability, or she may have an invisible learning disability that affects her only when she attempts certain types of work. *What to do:*

○ Plan for most activities to be ones she can comfortably participate in.

○ For certain learning disabilities, the student may have a treatment plan that restricts the type and quantity of reading or writing she should do. Don't second-guess the parent or learning specialist; if you are uncertain about the suitability of an assignment, ask for feedback.

○ When you give assignments for students to work on at their desks, give her a related assignment that is adapted to her academic needs.

- Use a team format for games and review activities so that no one student stands out as the one who doesn't know the answers. (And be prepared for a surprise: Your special-needs student may be the one who knows her catechism better than anyone else.)
- Simplify activity instructions and present them clearly.
- Avoid situations that put your student on the spot or embarrass her because she can't keep up.
- Look for opportunities to draw on her strengths and share her talents with the class.

Be aware that learning disabilities, such as difficulty processing written words, difficulty with fine-motor tasks, or difficulty making sense of speech in a noisy environment can affect students of normal or high intelligence. Presenting the lesson material in more than one manner lets students focus their attention on the format that makes the most sense to them.

Regardless of the academic ability of your students, read aloud any written information that is essential for students to know. If students have just read a Bible passage silently, you the teacher should read it aloud before you begin discussion. If the class is working through a written study guide, you the teacher should read aloud each question before giving the answer. If students take turns reading aloud, either call on volunteers who can read clearly and well, or plan to repeat and rephrase what was just read by the student.

The Student With a Physical Disability

This could be a student with a significant permanent disability, but most of the comments that follow apply to students with minor or temporary injuries as well. Small acts of thoughtfulness, born from a spirit of collegiality, can dramatically improve your student's enjoyment of your class.

Resist any temptation to make a clever comment or joke. At best you are going to think up a line that your student has already heard thirty times. At worst, you'll say something really dumb and forever be remembered as The Catechist Who Said Something Really Dumb. Just because a student has an unusual or striking condition does not mean you need to "think of something to say." The proper things to say to a student presenting with a disability are: "Hello," "How are you today?" "I'm glad to see you," "We're going to have a good class today." In other words: exactly the same things you say to all your other students.

Don't be so inspired and amazed all the time. Refrain from describing your student as "inspiring" unless he did, in fact, inspire you to take up some particular course of action. ("Ben, hearing you tell me about your tennis tournament reminded me how much I used to love to play. I got out to the courts this weekend and had a great time.") When a student uses an alternative means to accomplish a normal, everyday task, this is usually just a case of being a regular person doing everyday things. Save congratulations for situations that are in fact noteworthy personal achievements.

It can be hard at times to be sure whether a disabled student needs help with a particular task or is just going about it in his usual, if unconventional, way. If you are uncertain, just ask. Stay focused on the planned classroom activities. Ask specific questions as they arise, in a casual, friend-to-friend manner: "Would you like me to get your books for you or do you prefer to do that yourself?" "We have a writing assignment planned. Is there anything in particular I need to help you with, or are you good to go?" It is not necessary or desirable to get a medical history or find out a million details unrelated to what is planned for class time.

If your student needs physical assistance, **listen carefully and**

follow directions exactly. Your student knows his body best and has long experience with what does and does not help. If you don't follow your student's instructions precisely, one or both of you may end up injured. Keep in mind your own limitations as well; ask for an aide to handle any tasks that are beyond your ability to manage safely.

Once you have an idea of your student's needs and abilities, make minor adjustments as appropriate to make the class more comfortable for your student. Have your student test for you to verify that seating arrangements are workable:

- **If your student has a hearing disability**, set up classroom activities so he can follow the entire class and participate fully. Repeat questions and answers from other students, if there is a chance your student was unable to understand what was said. (This is a good practice regardless of whether hearing impairments are a concern—it confirms you have understood what students are trying to say.)

- **If your student has a visual impairment**, narrate any purely visual cues during class. If you ask for a show of hands on who would like to play All Saints Bingo, out of courtesy to your student who can't see the other hands, just say, "I see five, six—make that eight hands in favor of bingo...." When you write information on the board, read it aloud.

- **If your student uses a wheelchair**, confirm there is adequate room for movement and space to turn around. Avoid situations that exclude or draw excess attention to your student, such as having everyone else sit on the floor when he cannot or everyone else squeeze into a tight space where the wheelchair won't fit. Rearrange furniture so your student can sit in the regular seating area rather than being relegated to a "special spot" in no man's land.

Don't assume that your student dislikes or can't play particular sports or games. Discuss your plans with your student and figure out how to set up a planned game in a way that he can participate. If you are surprised by the arrival of a student with a disability at an event where a particular activity was already planned and put into place, take a moment to ask the student how he would like to handle the situation. He might choose to:

○ Do the activity as planned with whatever adaptations are his usual method.
○ Have an assistant help him by doing some or all of the physical task, but under his direction.
○ Modify the activity during his turn so that it better suits his abilities.
○ Participate in an alternate role, such as refereeing or score-keeping.
○ Sit this one out.

If you are habitually setting up games or activities that are unpleasant for your student, you're doing something wrong! Consider meeting with the student and parents to get some help. You might say, "I'm trying to develop some fun learning activities for our class. Can you help me with planning so we can come up with something good that everyone will enjoy?"

Invisible Disabilities Are Real Disabilities

You often cannot see someone else's physical pain, lack of sensation, hearing loss, blurry vision, muscle weakness, poor coordination, shortness of breath, or intense fatigue. If a student—any student —is reluctant to engage in a particular activity, respect that decision. She may share with you a reason for her choice, or she may not wish to discuss it.

In the religious-education setting, it is never the role of the catechist to second-guess a student's reported symptoms. When someone complains of a problem but has no apparent symptoms, do not assume the person is being lazy, rebellious, or attention-seeking. Students (and fellow volunteers) may choose to push themselves physically for some tasks but are silently operating at the limits of their abilities. It is very easy for someone to "look healthy" despite significant health problems. It is possible your class is so enjoyable a student is willing to endure a certain amount of pain just to be there.

It is prudent to confirm that parents are aware of the situation, especially if there is reason to think a student has an undiagnosed injury or illness. Parents may also be able to provide suggestions on how to include the student, especially if the student is too shy to discuss the particulars himself. Affirm for parents that you are happy to have the student participate in class at whatever level the student chooses.

○○○

The Church is a sacred community. Over the past several chapters, we've examined ways to share the faith with every student who comes to your class, regardless of age, ability, or academic background. You've gotten some ideas for activities you might like to include in your class plans and how you might put together a course that is helpful to the students who will soon be coming your way. Next let's look at how to work with one other important group of people in your faith-education community: your fellow volunteers.

7

CLASSROOM LEADERSHIP

Classroom discipline requires strong leadership. When working with other adults, it's easy to get sucked into the Leadership Vacuum —each teacher expecting the other to take charge. Class stalls, misbehavior is dealt with erratically, everyone gets frustrated, and no one knows how to fix it. Strong communication and advanced planning are the solutions. Sit down with your fellow volunteers and hold a pre-planning conversation. Here are some questions to help you and your co-catechists develop a leadership strategy.

What Role Would You Like to Play in This Class?

When there are multiple adults in the room, there are many ways to divide the workload. Here are some possible choices:

- ❍ One teacher leads class, the other adult takes purely supportive roles.
- ❍ The main teacher leads most of the class and the second adult leads one or a few activities.
- ❍ Catechists split the teaching work evenly within the class period.
- ❍ Catechists alternate class sessions—one leads this week, the other leads the following week.

If there is a student who needs one-on-one assistance, the adult who works best with that student should be free from other responsibilities during the one-on-one time. Don't assume the student's parent should be the one to provide the additional help, even if the parent is one of the classroom volunteers.

What Are You Good At and What Do You Love to Do?

There's no law that all catechists must teach every type of classroom activity. No sane person would ask me to lead music, if there's a competent musician somewhere in the room. It rarely occurs to me to tell the kids a story from my personal life, yet I've worked with catechists who excel at teaching this way. Some of these discoveries happen by surprise—my partner says she'd like to lead a prayer service, and when she does we realize, *Wow! She has a gift for this!* We make a point in the future to include more of this or that in our class plans. Finding out what you each enjoy lets you share the teaching load in a way that is more satisfying for everyone.

What Do You Want to Include in the Class Time?

This is a bit different than the previous question. We're focusing here not on what each of us wants to do ourselves but on what we want someone, anyone, to do. I like to put this question after the "talents" question because in learning about my partners' talents, I may think of class ideas I otherwise would not have attempted. I might think our class needs a good ice-breaker game, even though I myself am terrible at thinking up such things. Another catechist might want to study the lives of saints but not really know how to do it; that's a topic I enjoy teaching. We each make our wish list of classroom activities, then work together to figure out a plan for how to include the most important ones.

Do You Want to Modify the Pre-Planned Curriculum in Any Way?

When I am teaching on my own, I can adapt course plans from my teacher's manual as needed and write up the modified class outline for myself. If I am working with another catechist, then we need to map out in advance what changes we are planning and make sure we understand how the class will progress.

Don't be nervous about approaching your co-catechist with ideas for changes. Teachers usually agree about what elements of the curriculum need to be modified for their class. It is much better to have this conversation before class begins than to suffer through a plan you were afraid to customize. Alternately, your fellow volunteer may want to stick to the course plans as written but may propose ideas on how to work through the problems you anticipated.

Put It in Writing!

Writing out your plans helps you organize, communicate, and keep your class on track. When you are new to teaching a particular kind of class, write out your plans in painful detail. With time and experience, you will be able to build outline-type plans that are just enough to remind you of the overall framework for the class.

When working with a partner, at the very least you need an activity-by-activity list of who does what when. Here's a sample from a year I co-taught fifth grade with another experienced catechist:

Opening: Karen takes attendance, Jen supervises worksheets

Opening prayer: Karen

Start lesson: Jen

Pause to show kids item Karen brought from home that goes with lesson: Karen

Finish lesson: Jen

Class discussion: Karen

Announcements: Jen

More announcements: Karen

Closing prayer: Karen

Dismissal: Jen (Karen has to be in the parking lot early to help with traffic control.)

Using this outline/plan, we can each then take our assigned parts and build as detailed a set of notes as we need for our portion of the class.

Time Management

If multiple instructors are taking turns teaching during the same class period, it's easy to run into time-management problems. I might get carried away with answering questions and leave my partner short on time for teaching her portion of the class. Discuss this possibility in advance and make a backup plan. Which portions of the class can be compressed or skipped if need be? Should the co-teacher keep track of time and give a two-minute warning? A courtesy during class is to ask your partner how to proceed: "Kids, we're about out of time for questions. Miss Karen, what do you think? Should we take two more questions or should we move on to our next activity and come back for questions next time?" If you are the one waiting your turn, observe student cues. If students are actively engaged and excited about their current activity, it may be wise to let it run a little longer than planned to take advantage of the class momentum.

Rehearsals

It is not necessary to rehearse every word you'll ever say in class. When working with a team, however, there are a few types of activities that do require practice runs:

○ **Scripts.** Any volunteers who need to act from a script (whether read, memorized, or improvised) deserve a chance to rehearse until they can perform smoothly and comfortably. Even those with no speaking parts need at least one run-through.

○ **Games.** Walk your helpers through the game at least once, making sure they understand how the game works and what their role will be. You do not want to be explaining your clever obstacle course to your helpers while thirty second-graders wait impatiently for the fun to begin.

○ **Complex prayer services.** Take a few minutes to walk through the plan—I'll light the candles and dim the lights, she's going to start with an opening prayer, students will stand here, my speaking part begins there, it will all finish up with this and then that.

Practice and planning sessions don't need to be long and exhausting. Just make sure all participants have a clear understanding of what they need to do and how to do it.

Silent Discipline Help

If it is my turn to lead the class, it is my responsibility to manage the classroom. I need to be the leader. I need to be the one who pauses to address an emerging discipline problem. It is not fair to expect my partner to interrupt my lesson in order to deal with a disruptive situation.

When my partner is teaching, the best help is silent help. I can stand next to the chatty pair in the back corner or silently pick up the note being passed around the table. If a student needs to be moved, I can quietly rearrange without interrupting the lesson in progress.

Discuss your planned discipline strategy with your teaching partners before class begins. The act of describing your ideas to each other is a powerful communication tool. During class you will need to respond to unexpected situations; having already established a general approach gives you a foundation on which to improvise with confidence.

With time and experience, my partners and I will work out some ways to communicate and share responsibilities so that classroom discipline becomes increasingly effortless. But at the beginning, explicit conversations and detailed planning help ensure there is always effective leadership in the classroom.

8

BUILDING YOUR
OWN CLASS PLANS

We've looked at how to plan a "typical" class, but you need to plan *your* class. Here's a step-by-step method to help you think about what you want to include and figure out a workable way to put it all together.

STEP #1

Pre-Planning Questions

Your teacher's manual, other educational resources you have on hand, and your own creativity will together give you many ideas about how to teach your class. Use some basic "about the class" questions to decide what activities are best to include:

❍ When will students arrive? Will they arrive all at once or will they arrive individually over a period of time?

❍ What are the goals for my class? Are there songs or prayers we need to learn or particular facts students need to master? Is there a type of spirituality that students need to discover?

❍ What are the most effective activities for helping my students achieve these goals?

❍ How much time do I have?

❍ How old are my students? What kinds of activities are best suited to the range of personalities I expect? What types of activities will be too boring, distracting, or confusing for these students?

○ What combination of activities will help ensure that all students benefit from at least a portion of my class?

○ How will dismissal take place? Do I need to plan an activity for the dismissal time? What do we need to do to get ready for dismissal?

I'm looking for two big red flags as I answer these questions:

1. Class activities that aren't a realistic fit for the time, space, students, or resources we actually have on hand.
2. Activities that would be great fun but don't add anything to the lesson.

Of all your possible activity ideas, identify the ones that are the best fit for the needs of your class.

STEP #2

Create an Activity Wish List

Make a list of the activities you would like to include in your class. It is helpful to write each activity on an index card or slip of paper. For each activity, decide:

○ Is this activity quiet or loud? Messy or neat?

○ Where will my students work on this activity?

○ What supplies or setup time is required? What is the process for finishing this activity, including cleanup, so that we can move on to the next activity?

○ How much time is required? Note the estimated amount of time on your wish-list notes.

Put Together the Plan

Write up a possible rhythm for the class and see if it "works." Is there a natural progression, or flow, from one activity to another? Does the first activity get the class ready for the second? Does the second finish with students ready to easily transition to the third? Can all the activities be completed in the amount of time you have? If you've used index cards or sticky notes, you can physically rearrange the list as many times as needed. Keep reorganizing until you think you have a plan that meets your goals.

Walk It Out

Your mind makes plans, your body verifies. Physically go to the space where your students will have class and move from location to location, just as your students will. Be as detailed as possible: When students walk in the door, what will they do first? Check in at the front table? Find a seat? Grab a textbook off the shelf?

You are looking for traffic jams, temptations, missing supplies, excessive transitions, and stuff like, "How do I dim these lights?" If you can't *prove* that the DVD player works, *and that it will still be in the room come class time*, assume you aren't going to have use of it. Remember that catechists are subject to the same laws of physics as everyone else—you can't be in more than one place at a time. Don't plan to lead the class in song, fill out the attendance sheet, and take preschoolers to the bathroom all at the same time.

If your classroom will be used for other events in-between your class sessions, you may not be able to set up the room exactly how you want it. During your walk-through, make a checklist of last-minute preparations you'll need to do when you arrive to teach.

STEP #5
Make Adjustments

Allow enough time for your on-site visit that you can pause to rearrange and retest your plan as needed. Revise your plan until you think you have a simple, manageable class-time plan.

STEP #6
Create Your Backup Plans

Ask yourself:

○ What are the most important facts from the lesson for this class?
○ What will I do if this craft takes longer than I thought, or this game goes more quickly than I expected?
○ If we end up with a delay or interruption, what activities can I skip in order to leave time for the most important elements of class?

When you're in the middle of teaching and disaster strikes, your memory is likely to fail. Write down your list of backup activities and keep it on hand for when you need to make last-minute changes. Get in the habit of carrying around a file folder with fun extra assignments that you can pass out at a moment's notice.

STEP #7
Try It Out!

You won't really know how your plan works until it's time for class. Prepare as best you can, then put on a big smile and go for it.

If you run into trouble during class, don't panic. Think on your feet to problem-solve surprises. I don't think I've ever had a class run exactly how I thought it would, but I've had lots of great classes. Planning isn't teaching. Planning is the tool that prepares you to teach the class you need to teach as well as can be hoped under the circumstances that come your way.

STEP #8
Make More Adjustments

You tried out your plan and you may have run into one or two problems. What can you do differently to improve your class?

Sometimes you will need several class sessions to know whether your plan is workable or not. You may find that the first time you had to initially skip or modify an activity, but that the following class runs more smoothly, and your original plan works just fine. Or you may find that class after class there is not enough time or that students do not respond well to a planned activity. In that case, drop or change the activity to better meet the needs of your students.

STEP #9
Try It Again

Teaching is a skill that develops over time with practice and experience. Don't give up on yourself just because you have a few rough classes. Even the most experienced teachers still have difficult days. If you are regularly struggling with the same problem, ask other teachers for ideas on how to improve your class. Be patient and persistent: It may take several tries and multiple strategies to problem-solve a difficult situation.

When Everything Goes Nuts

Sometimes you do everything right and your class still goes haywire.

One December, Linda and I, the two fifth-grade catechists, were manning the Saint Nicholas Room at our all-day Advent special event. Groups of about twenty students would arrive, take our class, and then move on to the next station.

It was going great. We quickly figured out a few improvements to our plans to make the class run more smoothly. We paid attention to our students' cues and made adjustments for each group as needed. The kindergartners loved it. The fifth-graders loved it. The second-grade girls ate it up.

And then a group of some two dozen eight-year-old boys showed up. And it was all over.

These were not ordinary eight-year-old boys. These were overtired, overtaught, restless, ready-to-run-on-the-playground eight-year-old boys. They arrived, and in moments the classroom transformed into a practice field for magic-marker swordsmanship. Someone needed to take charge, and fast.

We confiscated the markers.

We stopped everything and said an emergency "Our Father."

(Those boys can deliver an impressive "Our Father" when they discover you are serious!)

And then we completely changed the class.

The planned craft went home as homework. We pared down the scheduled lesson to the bare essentials, then went straight to our folder of backup activities.

It was a great class.

Not the class we had planned. But it was the class those boys needed that afternoon. They even learned about Saint Nicholas. Goal met.

A class gone bonkers doesn't mean you're a lousy teacher. It does mean you need to reassess and change gears. I make my plans and God makes his. When everything goes crazy, stop, take a deep breath, and quickly come up with a new plan.

CONCLUSION

BRINGING YOUR PASSION FOR CHRIST TO THE CLASSROOM

Teaching religious education can be overwhelming. Will I do a good job? Will the students care? Can someone like me possibly have something interesting to say to this younger generation? Everything is so different from when I was a kid! Don't be discouraged. There's some very good news:

**This is the most important subject
your students will ever study.**

We say "math is important" or "good nutrition is important," and certainly those are true. But there is literally no subject more exciting, more relevant, and more personally important to your students than God. Your students need good arithmetic skills for the next seventy years. They need God for all eternity.

The number-one thing you can do to make your class come alive for your students is to care about your faith. To love Jesus, and be desperate to share that love with others. To want to know more and more about God, and to want to share that knowledge with your students. To try to model your own life after the saints, and to want to show your students what holiness looks like so they, too, can fight the good fight day after day.

Students can sense when you take your faith seriously. *This matters. This is worth the sacrifice.* A commitment to your faith —despite the difficulties, despite the setbacks, despite the times when life is scary or overwhelming or just plain boring—speaks for itself. Students can sense your genuine passion for Christ and your love for each little soul who comes into your classroom.

What Gift Is Christ Calling You to Share Today?

Our love for Christ is not some mere feeling. We humans are body and soul, and we share our love not just with warm sentiments but through our actions. All the work of classroom management, the planning, the discipline, the learning how to respond to student problems? These efforts matter because we have a life-giving message, and it is important that the message not be lost amid chaos and distractions. My love takes on physical form, it is *embodied*, when I work to teach the best class I can.

When a class of mine goes wrong, I can usually pin it on one of a few things:

I didn't plan and prepare.

I wasn't paying attention to my students and responding to their needs.

I was trying to cram too much into the class.

I was trying to entertain rather than teach.

I was trying to be somebody else.

As a teacher and a Christian, I have certain things I'm good at and certain things I love. And then there's a whole lot of stuff that I just don't know very much about. The Lord knows who he is sending to my class today. He doesn't need me to know everything or be everything. I have to build my class around the tasks God gave me to do. There's another teacher who will have a turn at bringing to my students what I cannot.

How has God made you? What talents has he given you? You are God's work of art, made in his image, destined to share his love with the world in a way that no one else can.

You can learn to teach and to teach well. It is not always easy, and you'll rarely have a perfect day. But with God's help and some hard work, you can touch the hearts and souls of students longing to know Jesus. May God bless you in all that you do.

Other Liguori Publications Titles for
CATECHISTS...

Handbook for Today's Catechist
English #818462 • Spanish #818714

Offers guidance on speaking and living the faith as well as basic do's and don'ts associated with teaching the faith. Includes a lesson outline, a chapter on planning and preparing for lessons, practical helps for teaching Church tenets, and a discussion of the roles catechists play in their students' faith formation.

Handbook of Sacraments for Today's Catechist
English only #819469

Teachers, parents, and volunteers will love using this energetic, complete, and lively exploration of the seven sacraments. Excellent for use alone or as a supplement to the best-selling *Handbook for Today's Catechist.*

Handbook for Adaptive Catechesis
English only #821455

This comprehensive book covers the most-encountered special needs, strategies for having fruitful dialogues with parents, identifying students for your special-needs program, recruiting effective catechists and teachers, and developing lesson plans.

To order, visit Liguori.org, call 800-325-9521, or visit your local bookstore

Liguori Publications offers many titles as eBooks through leading distributors such as Amazon, Barnes & Noble, Kobo, and iTunes.